FIRST ON THE WALL

THE LAST WORD ON THE FIRST AMERICAN ADVISORS TO DIE IN VIETNAM

M/Sgt Ray Bows, US Army, Retired

FIRST ON THE WALL

M/Sgt Ray Bows, U.S. Army, Retired

ISBN: 0-929973-08-9

Bows & Company Publishing, PO Box 1865, New Smyrna Beach, Florida 32170

The author encourages comments and feedback. Email: vietnamlore@hotmail.com

Copyright © 2012 by Bows and Company - Lineage PWR. All rights reserved.

No part of this publication may be reproduced or transmitted in any form or by any means, electronic or mechanical, including photocopy, recording, or any information storage and retrieval system, without the permission in writing from the publisher.

Permission is only given for brief excerpts to be used for the purpose of reviewing this publication in newspapers, magazines, periodicals and bulletins, provided the source of the material used is acknowledged in each instance.

Book design by Pia Bows. Cover photographs (from left to right): Major Howard B. Boston, courtesy of LTC Victor W. Gorlinsky, U.S. Army (ret.); M/Sgt Chester M. Ovnand, courtesy of John Sheridan; Major Dale R. Buis, courtesy of Hon. J. Stephen Buis; LTC Victor W. Gorlinsky and the BIF Compound, courtesy of LTC Victor W. Gorlinsky, U.S. Army (ret.)

Other books by Ray Bows:

US & Allied Military Tokens of the Vietnam War, 1983
Vietnam Military Lore - Another Way to Remember, 1988
Vietnam Military Lore - In The Name of War, 1996
Vietnam Military Lore - Legends, Shadows and Heroes, 1997
Time-Line Vietnam - The Tiger That Ate The Firebase, 2004
In Honor and Memory - Installations and Facilities of the Vietnam War, 2014

Printed in the United States of America

Dedicated to

Major Dale R. Buis, U.S. Army,

assigned to MAAG 5, Song Mao

Master Sergeant Chester M. Ovnand, U.S. Army

Major Howard B. Boston, U.S. Army (ret.)

Major Jack D. Hallett, U.S. Army (ret.)

LTC Victor W. Gorlinsky, U.S. Army (ret.)

assigned to MAAG 7, Bien Hoa

and

Specialist James V. Buis, U.S. Army

My sincere thanks to members of the Buis family, including Kurt Buis; Honorable J. Stephen Buis; Major J. Errett Buis, U.S. Marine Corps; Gretchen Buis; to John Sheridan, nephew of M/Sgt Chester M. Ovnand; to Major Howard Boston, U.S. Army (ret.) and his wife, Ardys, and their son Robert Boston; to LTC Victor W. Gorlinsky, U.S. Army (ret.) and his wife Blanche; to Colonel Nathaniel P. Ward III, U.S. Army (ret.) and his son Captain Nathaniel P. Ward IV, US Army (ret.); to historians and Vietnam veterans Daniel R. Arant and Bruce Swander, whose input to this project was paramount; and to my wife, Pia, for her everlasting love, friendship and support.

Contents

1959
DALE R BUIS · CHESTER N OVNARD

Foreword

Between 1946 and 1960, there were forty-four United States military assistance advisory groups located around the world. MAAG Indochina, which later became MAAG Vietnam, was one of them. Over the years, stories, articles, and chronological summaries have made note of the 8 July 1959 communist-planned attack on the U.S. MAAG advisory compound at Bien Hoa, which took the lives of the first two American military advisors to die in Vietnam. Most narratives which have dominated available information on the raid have been found to be inaccurate or incomplete. While news services wrote their own slants on the attack, they based them on MAAG and South Vietnamese press releases at the time, which in themselves contained inaccurate information.

In 1959, news reporters had no time to investigate every aspect of the story, which was a passing one occurring in a foreign land few had heard of, and assumptions were made about missing details.

The circumstances of the deaths of Major Dale R. Buis and Master Sergeant Chester M. Ovnand would have passed into obscurity, if their names had not become the first two inscribed on the Vietnam Veterans Memorial in Washington, D. C. Since 1983, their names have been in such prominence that questions have been raised and hearsay has proliferated.

Although the attack on Bien Hoa was difficult to reconstruct historically, through Dan Arant and Bruce Swander additional information was discussed and compiled; and through Colonel Nathaniel Ward III, Captain Howard Boston and LTC Victor Gorlinsky, sharing their first hand recollections of the attack, this story is told.

Hopefully, this book will dispel the myth surrounding the deaths of the two advisors whose names are first on the Wall.

Ray Bows
M/Sgt US Army (retired)

Chapter 1
"When Legend Becomes Fact"

In the days of pith helmets and Bermuda shorts, MAAG advisors stand in front of the screened-in porch at the main building of the BIF Compound at Bien Hoa. From left to right - two advisors in tropical uniform whose identities cannot be confirmed, then MAAG 7 advisors Captain Edward Beau Turner, Captain Howard Boston, Major Charles Watson and Captain Victor Gorlinsky.
Photo courtesy of LTC Victor Gorlinsky, USA (ret.)

The date, 1959, inscribed on the Vietnam Veterans Memorial in Washington, DC, marks the year of the deaths of the first American advisors killed at the hands of the Viet Cong. That year also saw other unforgettable events which took place elsewhere in the world: in Cuba, Fidel Castro and his forces arrived in Havana; in France, General Charles De Gaulle was inaugurated as the first President of the Fifth Republic; in Hollywood, Walt Disney released his animated film *Sleeping Beauty*; in Clearlake, Iowa, a chartered airplane crash killed Buddy Holly, Richie Valens and "the Big Bopper" Jiles Perry Richardson, Jr.; at Cape Canaveral, separate launches of a Titan intercontinental ballistic missile and the Vanguard II weather satellite were deemed successful; while Alaska and Hawaii were admitted to the Union as the 49th and 50th States.

The year before, South Vietnamese President Ngo Dinh Diem had given the communist guerillas, previously known as the Viet Minh, a new name – the "Viet Cong". The 1958 term was derived from the words "Vietnam Cong San" meaning *Vietnam Communists.* A contemptuous term, it was a name intended to portray the brutal spirit of guerillas causing havoc in the South.

April 1958 had seen Diem reject a North Vietnamese proposal for the North and South to reduce troop numbers and to open trade relations. In retaliation of Diem rejecting the communist proposals, considered by the North as steps to unification, Viet Cong guerillas steadily increased their terrorist activities south of the 17th parallel.

Many of those activities involved killing at least one local South Vietnamese official a day, be it a village chief, a rural policeman, a district official, a priest, a nun, or a school teacher. School girls about to graduate were also targeted by the communists.

By June 1958, the communists formed a coordinated command structure in the eastern Mekong Delta. Then, in December, the Communist Party Central Committee decided to "open a new stage of the struggle" as the Viet Cong moved to overt insurgency.

On 4 February 1959, U.S. Army Special Forces officer Captain Robert D. McKnight stated:

> "An economical form of war is guerilla warfare which is a potent weapon that is adaptable to the battlefield with its characteristic dispersion, fluid fronts and isolation."

Guerilla warfare is a cut-rate method of waging war, as evidenced by reports during World War II. General Dwight D. Eisenhower said that Free French Forces, operating clandestinely in France, were the theoretical equivalent of fifteen divisions, a number that far exceeded their actual count of members. General Eisenhower's estimate was based on Free French activity, which occurred between 5 and 27 June 1944 when the French underground carried out 3,000 rail demolitions, cut major road systems, and disrupted Nazi wire communications. In accomplishing such missions, six

Nazi divisions, destined for the Normandy front, were delayed at a critical time in conjunction with the D-Day Invasion. Surprise depends on a combination of tactics and technique. Tactical decisions of guerillas are often based on the locations of enemy installations and intelligence information about the enemy. The communists in Vietnam were already prepared to use such basic tactics, and by May 1959 had finalized a plan to attack American military advisors working with South Vietnamese Army units.

By mid-1959, President Diem began reorganizing the South Vietnamese Army. Under the reorganization program, the 1st and 2d ARVN Field Divisions, logically, became the 1st and 2d ARVN Infantry Divisions; but the 3d ARVN Field Division became the 5th ARVN Infantry Division; the 13th ARVN Light Division became the 21st ARVN Infantry Division; and the 14th ARVN Light Division became the 22d ARVN Infantry Division. Diem hoped that giving existing units higher numerical designations would make it appear as though the total division strength in South Vietnam was being increased. Asked about the high numeric designations, U.S. MAAG Vietnam Commander Lieutenant General Samuel T. "Hanging Sam" Williams said that he wanted to "fool General Giap [in North Vietnam], at least for a little while, and keep him guessing," as to the South Vietnamese Army's actual strength. Yet the appearance of troop strengths being increased to combat communist insurgents, only further polarized the already tense situation which existed between the North and the South. Although these new divisions were designed to be superior in fire power to North Vietnamese Army units, with the intended purpose of quelling an invasion from the north, as had happened in Korea, the South Vietnamese units also had the mission of seeking out and destroying the Viet Cong in their jungle lairs. It became apparent that the divisions, dependent on artillery support, were not willing to venture beyond the firing range of their 4.2 inch mortars and 105mm Howitzers, thus, were road-bound to highways and major established routes.

Among such units was the former 4th ARVN Field Division, which was redesignated the 7th ARVN Infantry Division. The 7th was headquartered at Bien Hoa, located in the flatlands, twenty miles north-northeast of Saigon. The city was surrounded by rice paddies and spattered with coniferous trees and palms. The expansive Dong Nai River, which cut through Bien Hoa Province, played an important role in the province's livelihood, and for the first U.S. advisors sent to Bien Hoa, was a source of recreation for boating and water skiing. In later years, Bien Hoa would be a major hub with its expanded air base occupied by the U.S. Air Force and several U.S. Army installations, while the city itself became a G.I. town of seedy bars and whorehouses until 1968, when during the Tet Offensive the city was all but destroyed.

In 1959, Bien Hoa was still considered a lazy, insignificant village when compared to the hustle and bustle of Saigon. Its only American military inhabitants were the advisors to the 7th ARVN Division.

The year 1959 was not a time of U.S. Army uniforms associated with Vietnam in the later intense combat years of the war. It was considered a tropical assignment and advisors often wore khaki Bermuda shorts, knee-high socks, short sleeve open neck shirts and pith helmets - uniforms more associated with support troops in the China-India-Burma Theater during World War II, rather than Vietnam. The carrying of weapons by advisors was strictly forbidden by the MAAG Vietnam Commander General Samuel T. Williams.

Military Assistance Advisory Group (MAAG) had an unwritten policy that advisors would not forward any formal derogatory reports about South Vietnamese Army unit failures up the chain of command to MAAG Headquarters, where they could be seen by General Williams, who would, then, feel obligated to relay such reports to President Ngo Dinh Diem. The policy stuck in the craw of many advisors whom often wondered what their true purpose was in their mission to advise and correct discrepancies in South Vietnamese Army units. Lieutenant Colonel Bergen B. Hovell, a field grade advisor in I Corps, 2d Military Region, remembered his first Senior Advisors Conference in 1959:

> "I was shocked to hear some advisors reporting on a world I had never seen. A man from Mars listening to it would have believed that everything was going quite well . . . in substance we reported that while the unit we were working with was

probably as good, or better than comparable units, it couldn't really punch its way out of a paper bag... People were scared to death of General Williams . . . people were afraid to speak. You would have thought that General Williams would have wanted to know where the weaknesses and problems were, but nothing seemed to improve. The general was only concerned with training the divisions to meet an attack from North Vietnamese regulars if they invaded the South. He refused to recommend that the role of the ARVN Divisions be not only to fight the communists, but to become a combined action of pacification and hunting the Viet Cong," said Colonel Hovell. "He felt that the Vietnamese units would go stale guarding bridges and acting as policemen in the villages. None-the-less, there were close to a dozen fire fights in March and April between South Vietnam Forces and the Viet Cong. Then, in May, the Viet Cong took high ground just outside Bien Hoa and held it against a South Vietnamese Battalion."

Then, in a little over a month, the attack on the U.S. military advisory compound at Bien Hoa was reported:

"Daily Wireless File, United States Information Service, 39 Dao Lo Ham Nghi, Saigon - Thursday July 9, 1959. TWO MAAG PERSONNEL, TWO VIETNAMESE KILLED IN COMMUNIST ATTACK -

"SAIGON, July 9 - A band of communist terrorists last night attacked an American billet at Bien-Hoa, 20 miles north of here, during a movie showing, and killed two American military advisors. A Vietnamese soldier and a Vietnamese mess attendant were also killed in trying to repel the attackers. One of the communists was killed.

"A third American was wounded, while two other American military advisors were unharmed. The attack occurred shortly after 7 p.m.

"An explosive charge and small-arms, including automatic weapons, were used by the terrorists, estimated to number between five and ten. Vietnamese guards returned fire forcing the terrorists to flee.

"Names of the dead and wounded Americans, 'training advisors' to the Seventh Vietnamese Army Division, were withheld pending notification of next of kin. The third American, suffering a gunshot wound, was moved to Saigon and then evacuated to the Philippines. His condition is reported to be serious but not critical.

"Immediately after being notified of the attack, the Vice-President of Vietnam, Nguyen Ngoc Tho, the Secretary of State for the Presidency, Nguyen Dinh Thuan, and Secretary of State for the Interior, Lam Le Trinh, went to the scene from Saigon.

"President Ngo Dinh Diem, on a tour of Central Vietnam, has been informed."

This attack by communists, in which U.S. servicemen were killed, has become a point of focus at the Vietnam Veterans Memorial in Washington, DC. No visitor can descend the walkway and arrive at the apex of the Wall without noticing the date 1959, nor can anyone ignore the first two names the memorial bears – *Dale R. Buis* and *Chester N. Ovnard* (sic), the two regular U.S. Army soldiers killed on the fateful night of 8 July 1959. For years, the first name was almost always mispronounced as Bew-is. The correct pronunciation is *Bice* as in "ice". The inscription and spelling of the name "Ovnard" is, actually, Chester M. Ovnand, re-inscribed on panel 7E, again in error, as Chester A. Ovnand (with an 'A' rather than an 'M' middle initial). Such errors are minor compared to the misinformation about these two men killed in the second enemy attack on Americans in Vietnam. There had been a previous attack in 1957.

Master Sergeant Chester M. Ovnand's name, again re-inscribed incorrectly on panel 7E of the Vietnam Veterans Memorial in Washington, D. C. Pia Bows

The well planned and determined 1959 Viet Cong attack, orchestrated through a local communist cell, was premeditated many weeks in advance of its occurrence.

Second hand interviews, press releases, and reports after the attack, as well as conversations with General Samuel T. Williams, the MAAG commander, almost twenty-two years later, have distorted what actually happened at the advisory billet. By the time stateside editors of major newspapers condensed the original stories, readers would believe that two U.S. Army advisors watching the movie, *The Tattered Dress*, on a home movie projector were helplessly gunned down at Bien Hoa and died instantly. Such assumptions deviate from the actual facts.

President Dwight D. Eisenhower was two-and-a-half-years into his second term of office, when the raid on Bien Hoa occurred. At that time, I was a thirteen year old junior high school student who only became cognizant of the killings of the two advisors twenty-four years later, upon one of my first visits to the Wall after my retirement from the U.S. Army in 1983. Since then, for over thirty years, while researching the lives of Buis and Ovnand, I have had the privilege of interviewing and becoming friends with two of the men who were in the improvised movie theatre the night that Major Buis and Master Sergeant Ovnand fought for their lives.

The survivors interviewed were then captains Howard "Blackie" Boston of Blairsburg, Iowa, and Victor "Vic" Gorlinsky of Reston, Virginia. The details of the story of Buis and Ovnand are presented in this book, which addresses all the available facts, and certain assumptions which cannot be ignored. Victor Gorlinsky told me, "I don't want to split hairs with any reporters who wrote about the attack at the time, I'm sure they did the best they could, but the complete story has never been told."

All the details need presenting as an antidote to those stories that we were led to believe. "When the legend becomes fact, print the legend." So, goes the well known cliché from the movie *The Man Who Shot Liberty Valence.* This axiom may have been good enough for Ransom Stoddard and Tom Doniphon, played by Jimmy Stewart and John Wayne, but it is an injustice if this saying is allowed to be applied to the deeds of Major Dale Buis and Master Sergeant Chester Ovnand, because their conduct on the night of 8 July 1959 was much more than was reported. From the very beginning of the Vietnam War until its end, heroic actions of servicemen were played down in the press, after all, how can there be an unjust war with just, dedicated, and heroic men serving in it?

Even before Major Howard Boston and Lieutenant Colonel Victor Gorlinsky are introduced, through their own chapters in this book, the reader will be exposed to the views of events they witnessed, which are contradictory to what was reported at the time. Many of those discrepancies are explained in Boston's and Gorlinsky's own words.

Chapter 2
The Phantom Mail Box

Although press reports stated that there was a mailbox at the MAAG Compound in 1959, Victor Gorlinsky, who was the mail officer, is certain there was no mailbox at the BIF Compound during his tour. However, by 1963, the compound had a mail room in the building, previously occupied by the chief cook and his family who lived there when the compound was attacked on 8 July 1959. Photo by Ray Jewett, MAAG PIO (1963)

In 1987, when I began my research on the names on Panel 1E of the Vietnam Veterans Memorial in Washington, DC, I drew on published accounts of the events that transpired at Bien Hoa on 8 July 1959. At the time I compiled information from all the sources available to me. I was amiss at my attempt to weave a story which, I know now, was only partially fact and partially assumption on the part of reporters of the day. My 1988 story served its purpose for my book about military tokens and money used in Vietnam, but *Vietnam Military Lore 1959-1973...Another Way To Remember* contained a conclusion that should not have been drawn.

> "Major Buis arrived in Vietnam on 6 July 1959 and was assigned as the eighth member of the MAAG Advisory Team. Dale Buis was befriended by a Vietnamese boy of eight or nine years old who helped him settle in. The boy, who was the mess cook's son, was the age of Buis' eldest of three sons back in the United States."

Dale Buis was *not* the eighth member of the advisory team at Bien Hoa, nor had he arrived in country on 6 July, but had been in Vietnam much longer. He was only passing through and overnighting at Bien Hoa, after a trip to the U.S. Army medical dispensary in Saigon. The scenario was a way for me to introduce the cook's son, who was reported killed during the attack on Bien Hoa, as well as introducing Major Buis' son, Kurt, back home in California.

From the numerous 1959 press reports, through later articles written in the 1980's, although each contained some truth, none of the articles were completely accurate. These stories may have met the writers' need to report the events of the day, or to set up what was to come in Vietnam as they wrote about the war in retrospect, but each story distorted some of the circumstances that had occurred during the attack. Even if some details were considered trivia, all helped to embellish what had actually happened.

Over fifty years after the fact, addressing press reports point by point might seem hypercritical, however, if someone does not correct misleading reports made back then, those accounts will stand. They are available for public viewing in archives, on the Internet, in books, and magazine articles. This situation is compounded by the fact that Major Buis' and Master Sergeant Ovnand's military personnel files were destroyed at the St. Louis National Personnel Records Center on 12 July 1973, when a fire decimated the major portion of U.S. Army military records for the period from 1912 through 1959.

In 1988, I was reminded that the U.S. Army's NCO heritage is the underpinning of our military strength and, further, senior sergeants are the ones who transmit the Army's living story from generation to generation. I had never thought about responsibilities to my former military career as continuing, but since 1988, I have taken that challenge, and the task shared with my fellow NCO's, as a serious duty and a great adventure. If misinformation about soldiers is put forth, particularly those who because of their deaths cannot set the record straight themselves, and is allowed to go unchallenged, it becomes accepted fact and everyone becomes poorer for it.

It appears that only one American journalist was actually at Bien Hoa's BIF Compound on the morning of 9 July 1959, to report on the aftermath of the communist attack. He was news correspondent Stanley Karnow. It is certain that variations of his original report, published in magazines and newspapers of the day, all stem from his next day observations, made while he was reporting from Vietnam.

Karnow reported that he surveyed the bullet-pocked villa at Bien Hoa, while Victor Gorlinsky later commented, "I believe, that at least one reporter was there that next morning, particularly if he reported having seen the bullet holes in the walls, which were repaired and patched by Vietnamese workers by the afternoon of the 9th. There were thirty-eight bullet holes altogether. Most were level in a horizontal line across the room, although some were rather high on the wall."

Victor Gorlinsky learned years later that there was a clear reason for the, inordinately, high bullet holes which scarred the mess hall's interior, once he told me that a STEN machine gun was used. I discovered, from arms expert Mike Seuberling, former police instructor at the University of Miami, that STEN's had a tendency to rise erratically.

It is from initial following-day observations, press releases by official sources, and later interviews of MAAG officers who were in Vietnam at the time, which formed the basis for all that has been written about the attack since. However, there have been at least sixteen inaccuracies, appearing in accounts that mention the first attack at Bien Hoa. They are listed as follows:

<u>Observation # 1</u> – Over the years it has been reported that MAAG 7 at Bien Hoa had as little as five, and as many as thirteen, members advising the 7th ARVN Infantry Division.

There were actually eight advisors assigned to MAAG 7, with one slot unfilled. They were: Lieutenant Colonel Ellsworth Davis, the senior Infantry officer; Major James Hallett, Infantry; Major Charles Watson, Infantry; Major Willie Punt, Infantry, who had duties at Cap Saint Jacques; Captain Howard Boston, Artillery officer; Captain Edward Beauregard Turner, Engineer officer; Captain Victor Gorlinsky, Signal officer; and Master Sergeant Chester Ovnand, the detachment first sergeant. There were actually nine slots at MAAG 7. The slot of full-colonel, the senior advisor's position, was temporarily being filled by LTC Davis. The individuals who were present in the mess hall the night of the attack were Hallett, Boston, Gorlinsky and Ovnand, plus Colonel Clay and Major Dale Buis, for a total of six Americans who were fired upon. Colonel Clay and Major Buis were visitors from MAAG 5 at Song Mao.

<u>Observation # 2</u> – It has been stated in more than one report that Major Dale Buis had been at Bien Hoa two days, and "the steamy humidity of Vietnam was going to take some getting used to."

In fact, Major Buis *did not* arrive at Bien Hoa two days earlier, but rather, that afternoon. Moreover, he had been stationed at Song Mao, Binh Thuan Province (II Corps) since November 1958 and, by then, had certainly acclimatized himself to the extreme humidity of the country. He had been in Saigon because he was being tested and treated for problems he was having with his right kidney. "Colonel Clay," whose first name is unknown, was sharing a sedan and Vietnamese driver with Major Buis. That afternoon, they hurried to get back to MAAG 5 in Song Mao, but once on the road they realized the trip could not be completed before dark. They decided to overnight at the BIF Advisory Compound at Bien Hoa.

<u>Observation # 3</u> – In no less than two dozen stories it has been stated that just prior to the attack, Master Sergeant Chester Ovnand finished a letter to his wife in Copperas Cove, Texas, and dropped it in the mess hall mail box.

Victor Gorlinsky commented, "I was with Sergeant Ovnand all afternoon. We had dinner together and after that we set up the movie projector. If he had finished up a letter to his wife, I never saw him, although I know he wrote home to her very often. One thing is for sure, there was no mailbox in the mess hall. If Chet had finished writing a letter, he would have tossed it on the table with the other out going mail. We had no mail box in the main building or on the BIF Compound - of that, I am certain. I was the postal officer and it was my job to carry the mail to Saigon."

Observation # 4 – "The quarters were located one hundred yards from the river's edge, and was surrounded by a two-strand barbed-wire fence which had no alarm devices attached."

"Indeed, the quarters were located about a hundred yards from the river," said Gorlinsky, "but not only were there no alarm devices on the 'two-strand barbed-wire fence' – there was no fence at all! I was down by the river on several occasions, and I can assure you, there was nothing between the compound and the riverbank. The Dong Nai River, itself, was the compound's only barrier until after the attack, when a four-foot wire fence was installed and concertina wire was strung in the area a day later."

Observation # 5 – Several articles reported that just prior to the attack two of the American officers "drifted off" to play tennis.

For story simplicity, it sounded better that "two" men, not "one", went off to play tennis, but the only MAAG 7 member to grab his racket and hit the tennis court was Captain Beau Turner. The arithmetic of who was where, and accounting for three officers absent from the administrative building during the attack, could not be easily explained. While Beau Turner was in a tennis match with others who were not connected to MAAG 7, Lieutenant Colonel Ellsworth Davis and Major Charles Watson were in their individual quarters.

Observation # 6 – In several articles it was stated that the advisors were watching a Jeanne Crain movie entitled *The Tattered Dress,* on a home movie projector.

The "home movie projector" was actually a theatre style 16mm movie projector, allocated to the unit to show full length feature films, provided on a scheduled basis by the Armed Forces Motion Picture Service, which was established as a morale and welfare institution army-wide in 1920. No one had brought a "home" movie projector to Vietnam. It was part of the unit's TAD equipment and its operator required a license.

"We had movies when we could pick them up from Bien Hoa Air Base. They were provided no more than two or three times a week," said Vic Gorlinsky. "Sergeant Ovnand always operated the projector."

Observation # 7 – Some accounts state the movie began at 7:00 P.M., while others have the first reel coming to an end at that time.

According to Victor Gorlinsky, the first twenty minute reel came to an end at approximately 1850 hours, because the movie generally started nights at 1830 hours.

"The first reel would have ended just before 7 P.M., but the movie didn't start then," said Vic.

"The sun sank quickly that evening and there was no moon," Howard Boston recalled. "Funny, there's no dramatic change of seasons in Vietnam, being that close to the equator it gets dark at the same time, whether it's December or July. Sunrise and sunset were always constant, and once the sun set, darkness came shortly thereafter, and the movie always started on time."

Observation # 8 – "Minutes prior to the room erupting in gun fire, no one heard two of the enemy position and ready a French MAT submachine gun in the rear window of the mess hall."

Reports stated, "a French MAT machinegun" was used when it was established the raiders were equipped with a STEN 9mm machinegun fired through the back window. The two man scenario inferred the machinegun used was a belt fed one, which was not the case. It only took one man to fire either a MAT or a STEN.

There are some similarities between MAT-49 and STEN machine guns. Both fire 9mm rounds. The MAT-49 submachine gun was developed by the French arms manufacturer - *Manufacture Nationale d'Armes de Tulle (MAT).* In 1949 it was adopted by the French Army and was also used by the *Gendarmerie Nationale* (French National Police). Someone, therefore, assumed that 9mm casings found at the scene probably came from a MAT submachine gun developed by the French.

The MAT-49 could use a 32-round magazine which was similar to the STEN 32-round magazine. But the STEN was a somewhat older weapon. Over 4 million were made in the 1940's. The STEN was a family of British submachine guns used extensively by Commonwealth Forces during World War II and Korea. The French knock-off of the STEN was the *Gnome et Rhoine* R5, which was manufactured by the motorbike and airplane manufacturer SNECMA. The French model came with a forward pistol grip and wooden, rather than a fold-out stock.

The difference is that while the MAT-49 has a slight tendency to rise, the STEN rises dramatically, and to the left, particularly while in the hands of an untrained user. The STEN's significance accounts for the high bullet holes that Vic Gorlinsky saw in the far wall, and is explored in more detail in Chapter 5 - Hanging "Hanging Sam*"*.

Observation #9 - It was reported that the three Americans not wounded could see the attacker's faces peering in through screen windows as bullets smashed into the floor and walls.

"This was not true," said Vic Gorlinsky. "Although some rounds may have hit low, there was just no way that any of us could see any of the faces of our attackers. We were too busy hugging the floor. It was just too dark, and things happened too fast for that to be possible. Besides, the screens and louvered windows shielded the VC from our view. When they started chopping away at us, the last thing we were concerned with was their faces."

Observation #10 - Reports have Major Buis and Master Sergeant

Ovnand being instantly slain, while other accounts state they died within minutes.

Major Buis and Sergeant Ovnand were not killed instantly. It will become clear that Master Sergeant Ovnand performed two quick thinking, extraordinary, and critical acts after he was hit by two 9mm rounds. Of equal importance, we will see that the unarmed Major Buis traveled approximately twenty feet, to confront an enemy sapper attempting to breach the mess hall with explosives.

Observation #11 – In a variety of reports it was said that two South Vietnamese guards were killed, while others have the number at three, and an eight-year-old Vietnamese boy, the mess cook's son, who had been watching the movie through a side window was either dead or laid dying.

Two Vietnamese soldiers were killed in the attack - one was a security guard, while the other was assigned as a kitchen helper.

The actual fate of the mess cook's eight year old son was more complicated than that of "dead or dying". The boy had been hit three times in the chest by enemy fire. Many reports confused his fate after the attack. This is explored in Chapter 14.

Observation #12 – At least one report had one of the terrorists, "who tried to throw a homemade bomb, into the room, miscalculate and blow himself up instead."

This issue was not about the Viet Cong sapper "miscalculating" but as we shall see, it was about him being confronted by Major Buis, who was unarmed.

Observation #13 – Accounts had Major James Hallett leaping across Master Sergeant Ovnand's body to turn off the lights inside the "sawmill" building, saving himself and three others by obscuring them in darkness.

It is certain that Major Hallett *did not* "leap over Chester Ovnand's body to turn off the lights." Hallett was sitting on a sofa, which he and Colonel Clay (visitor from MAAG 5) had positioned catty-corner to better see the screen before the movie started. Between where Major Hallett and Colonel Clay were sitting and the light switch on the back storeroom wall, another sofa, occupied by captain's Boston and Gorlinsky, was in a direct obstructive line to the light switch. Sergeant Ovnand did not go down when he was hit, but rather took the best possible action to protect his fellow advisors in the building, which was a role, erroneously, given by the press to Major Hallett. As we will see, Ovnand's body was not lying on the ground floor. It was found at the top of the stairs.

Observation #14 – At least one report had communist terrorists slipping into the building during the movie and exploding a bomb which killed two U.S. military advisors, the sapper himself and three South Vietnamese. Then following the bomb attack, other members of the terrorist band opened fire from outside the billet with small arms and automatic weapons. While Vietnamese Army guards returned fire "forcing the terrorists to flee to the nearby river from where they had come." Further, the story stated that the South Vietnamese killed, were two army guards and an attendant who tried to prevent the terrorist from exploding the bomb, while another terrorist had slipped into the building with the bomber, but escaped before the bomb went off.

No communist terrorists "slipped into the American military billet!" No sapper entered the main building at Bien Hoa, and the reported "attendant" who tried to prevent the terrorist from exploding his bomb was one of the U.S. Army advisors - Major Buis. The story stated the bomb was thrown first, then attackers opened fire which was the exact opposite of what actually happened! This report added fifty percent to the South Vietnamese casualty figures and had gotten who did what to whom all wrong. I thought to myself,

It was almost as if someone had been reading Ian Fleming's 1953 James Bond novel, Casino Royale, *in which two Bulgarians, wearing dark out-of-place suits and Panama-style straw hats got their lines and their bombs crossed. In a scheme to kill James Bond, two camera cases were given to the two Bulgarian agents, who were told that one case was the explosive and the other contained a very powerful smoke-bomb. Not knowing that they themselves were to be eliminated, they were instructed to throw the explosive bomb first, then disappear in a cloud of thick white smoke after detonating the second smoke-bomb case. The Bulgarians decided to take no chances and touched-off, what they thought was the smoke bomb first, killing themselves in a massive double explosion while leaving James Bond unharmed.*

The reporter who put the bomb exploding before the firing started, got his story just as ass-backwards as did the two Bulgarians, although he came away from his tale of the attack on Bien Hoa just as unscathed as did Double-O-Seven.

"Vietnamese Army guards returned fire, forcing the terrorists to flee to the nearby river from which direction they had come," was certainly the South Vietnamese version of what had happened because even though after South Vietnamese Army officers heard the firing nearby, their only action was to get word to ARVN headquarters. It took armed ARVN soldiers about fifteen minutes to get to the BIF Compound, and by then the communists were long gone.

The statement, "Another terrorist who had slipped into the building with the bomber escaping before the bomb went off" was pure fantasy. No sapper ever breached the main building!

Observation #15 – In 1985, Ronald H. Spector wrote on the subject stating, "Two young women from the nearby town had occasionally attended the movie as guests. (It was later alleged that the two were Viet Cong agents.)"

Three documents were used to write that commentary in *Advise and Support: The Early Years*, (1) a recorded 30 August 1979 interview conducted with Colonel Ernest P. Lasche, who was a member of MAAG headquarters in January of 1960; (2) USARPAC Weekly Intelligence Summary, 13 July 1959; and (3) a CIA Current Weekly Intelligence Summary, dated 16 July 1959.

"As far as the CIA Weekly Intelligence Summary dated 13 July

1959, I'm pretty confident as to where it came from," said Victor Gorlinsky. "We had a CIA agent that showed up a few days after the attack. He apparently tried to dress like a soldier and pretended he was one, but his facade was pretty transparent. He asked a lot of questions but he didn't get the answers that he wanted. He was grasping at straws and wanted the attack to be some cloak and dagger inside job. He was pretty comical, but, of course, we saw right through his disguise, while all the time, we tried to keep straight faces when dealing with him."

LTC Victor Gorlinsky continued, "As far as the statement about the two young women from a nearby village attending the movie as guests, and that later it was alleged they were Viet Cong agents, probably the best word for that scenario would be – Poppy-Cock! In addition to being the postal officer, I was also the mess officer and did my job well. I knew who came and who went through our mess hall. Although we had a couple of women who were cleaners, they always left BIF before 1600 hours. The only other woman who was ever in the mess hall was LTC Clark E. Burner's wife. LTC Burner was our MAAG Signal officer, and on one occasion, when he traveled from Saigon to Bien Hoa to Vung Tau, he brought his American born wife along, whose nickname was 'Clarkie' which was very similar to her husband's actual name. They stopped by MAAG 7 on the way to Cap Saint Jacques and Mrs. 'Clarkie' Burner sat in the mess hall and had a cup of coffee. Other than the two cleaning women, Mrs. Burner was the only woman who ever stepped through the doors of my mess hall. No Vietnamese women were ever in the main building watching a movie or otherwise – and I doubt seriously, if Mrs. 'Clarkie' Burner was a Viet Cong agent."

Observation # 16 - (1) One article made the assumption that because there was more than one movie reel, the entertainment that night must have been double feature movies. Generally, a full feature movie took between 4 and 6 reels of celluloid and there was only one feature movie shown that night. (2) Then it was stated that "insurgents had opened fire along the camp perimeter" which was not the case. (3) Major Buis was depicted as the more experienced of those there, while three of the others were also World War II Infantry veterans who had seen combat in Europe or the Pacific.

(4) It was reported that Buis "ordered the other soldiers to run upstairs and gather their weapons". Major Buis was not in a position to give orders. He was a guest at MAAG 7, was out-ranked, and he would have been aware that no one possessed authorized firearms. (5) The story suggests that "possibly" enraged Vietnamese nationalists pre-positioned a "time-bomb" before the attack. This diminished the communists role, inferred that Americans had no business in South Vietnam which upset nationalists, and that the sappers were capable of setting a bomb to explode several hours in advance. (6) The reporter had Major Buis losing "most of his head" when the bomb exploded. He did not die in that manner. Such an unconfirmed report, without verification, was irresponsible journalism.

In the early 1980's when the Vietnam Veterans Memorial was being planned, built, and dedicated, other accounts appearing in newspapers and journals across the nation gave mention to the attack on Bien Hoa. Various journalists interviewed some of the survivors of the attack, yet also got parts of the Buis/Ovnand story incorrect, although their goals seemed to have been to correct previous errors.

Examining more inaccurate reports, I asked myself, *what can be believed and what should be discounted?* Even if the circumstances in one account seemed credible and confirmed by another story, they could not be believed because some writers had taken information from accounts that had previously contained bad information.

Chapter 3
Meet the Real Boston Blackie

Staff Sergeant Howard "Blackie" Boston, U.S. Army, wearing a 4th Armored Division patch upon his return from World War II, stands with his father, Walt, on their Iowa farm. Photo courtesy of Robert Boston

The first time I talked to Howard Boston in 1993, he described himself as an "Iowa farm boy" who spent over twenty years in the Army, in the armor and artillery corps. After his retirement, he settled back in the Hawkeye State on his family's homestead with his wife, Ardys, who he had married in 1939, while their five children lived at various locations nearby. At one point in his army career, Howard acquired the nickname "Blackie" because of Jack Boyle's radio and TV character Boston Blackie. Initially, Howard was known as "Blackie Boston," but by 1959, during his Vietnam tour, LTC Ellsworth Davis, the acting commander of MAAG 7, came right out and called Howard - "Boston Blackie" as a matter of habit. Such nicknames were not unusual and superior officers would sometimes take such liberties with their subordinates, provided a nickname was not offensive, and soon Howard was known to many as "Boston Blackie."

First Contact

If Howard Boston and Vic Gorlinsky had not been sitting together, watching a movie at the BIF Compound at Bien Hoa on the night of 8 July 1959, or even if they had never met, they would still have a lot in common. From my first individual contact with each of them, they were both easy to talk too, proud of their military service, and interesting, courteous conversationalists. I thought it amazing that they would have discussions with me when I called them out of the blue and started asking a lot of questions about two soldiers with whom they had been stationed. There is no other way to describe Howard and Vic, other than a couple of great U.S. Army officers, who could not do enough to set the record straight on the deaths of Master Sergeant Chester Ovnand and Major Dale Buis. After reading his name in one story about the attack, I located Howard Boston in 1993, by asking *Information* for his telephone number in several Iowa cities.

Initially, it only took a few minutes before Howard and I were speaking to each other as though we were old army buddies, and although I was never able to meet Howard face to face, we became good friends over the phone. Back then, Howard and I would talk at least two or three times a week, for months and months, as I asked him never ending questions about MAAG 7, and every detail imaginable about the night of 8 July 1959 and its aftermath.

Each time I would call Howard, he was always outside. His wife, Ardys, would say something like, "Ray, he's puttering around out back," or "he's out mowing the lawn, hold on," or "I don't know what he's up to now, but I know where to find him."

In the course of our first of many conversations Howard told me, "I'd been in Vietnam since May 1959. I was training South Vietnamese soldiers in the use of howitzers, mortars, and supposedly how to speak English." Boston emphasized that as long as my story was about Major Buis and Master Sergeant Ovnand he would help in any way he could. I knew then, which would be reaffirmed sixteen years later, that like Vic Gorlinsky, Howard Boston was a modest man, never bragging, always conservative. He mentioned several times that Master Sergeant Ovnand and he were good friends, even though they were officer and enlisted. "We were a tiny family there at Bien Hoa," he said. "Sergeant Ovnand was a real nice fellow. We used to pitch horseshoes as a pastime."

Despite his reluctance to talk about himself, I prodded Howard all I could about his own service, then it would come to a point where he would say, "Okay, Sarge, let's get back onto the subject – Major Buis and Sergeant Ovnand. I've got too much to do around the house to be talking about myself. It's about them, not me, so I'll answer all the questions that are pertinent to your research..."

Both Armor and Artillery

It was not until March 2012 that I learned more about the officer whom I had come to know officially as U.S. Army Major Howard B. Boston, the man known to most of his associates as "Boston Blackie". He was born in Iowa on 6 February 1922. During World War II, as a soldier, he attended the U.S. Naval Amphibious School, and then participated in three campaigns in the European Theater. On 25 March 1944, as a staff sergeant, he was assigned to Company A, 10th Armored Infantry Battalion, 4th Armored Division. His division landed at Utah Beach on 13 July 1944, entering combat on 17 July at Coutances, France, which his unit took by 28 July 1944, after eleven days of hard fighting. Boston fought across France with the 4th Armored Division from Brittany to Orléans, as his unit suffered mixed fortunes in numerous tank battles. Midway across France, the 4th was directed to assemble in the Luxembourg area, in response to the German Ardennes Counter-offensive (the Battle of the Bulge) and after more heavy fighting, they entered Bastogne on 27 December 1944, during the Nazi siege. Boston later crossed into Germany with his unit over the Pruem River, saw Bitburg and reached the Rhine River on 8 March 1945. Crossing the southern portion of Germany, Company A of the 10th Armored Infantry withdrew to reserve on 19 April 1945, but attacked again on 6 May 1945, through the Regen and Freyung passes in Czechoslovakia. After nineteen months of almost non-stop fighting, Howard Boston was given home leave and travel time, only to find himself assigned halfway around the world to the 7th Infantry Division in Seoul, Korea. He began his new duties on 20 November 1945.

Between June 1947 and November 1948 Staff Sergeant Howard Boston was a member of the 7th Infantry Division's elite Palace Guard assigned to Duc Soo Palace, Seoul, Korea. Photo courtesy of Robert Boston

Honor Guard to OCS

A few days after the Japanese had surrendered aboard the USS *Missouri* in Tokyo Harbor on 2 September 1945, the 7th Infantry Division moved to Korea to accept the surrender of the Japanese Army at Seoul. After peace was declared, the 7th Division served as an occupation force in Korea and Japan. Then the division was cut in strength by one half, but remained on occupation duty patrolling Korea's 38th parallel where the country was split in two. In February 1947, a special honor guard unit was authorized performing duty as sentinels at Duk Soo Palace in Seoul, the meeting place of the United States and Soviet Union Joint Commission on Korea. The sixty man detail was also designed to provide honor guard duties for special events of the 7th Infantry Division, and furnish security for the home of the deputy commander of the division. The criteria for selection for members of "the Palace Guard" were strict and were based on military bearing, physical characteristics, and education. Staff Sergeant Boston was selected as one of the guard unit's first members. In June 1947, he made up part of the escort for the U.S. delegation during a meeting of the commission in Pyongyang, North Korea. He remained with the unit until it was inactivated on 19 November 1948.

After Howard Boston's return to the United States, he was recommended for Officers Candidate School and attended at the Infantry School, Fort Benning, Georgia, beginning on 14 March 1951. He received his commission on 8 July 1951, exactly eight years to the day before the Bien Hoa attack. As an officer, he took on assignments including gunnery officer, recon officer, company commander, liaison officer, and battery commander, at units in such places as Camp Atterbury, Indiana; Des Moines, Iowa; Fort Carson, Colorado; and with the 110th Infantry and 47th Infantry in Ulm, Germany. Then on 22 May 1959, Captain Boston was assigned as the artillery advisor to the Advisory Detachment, 7th ARVN Infantry Division, MAAG Vietnam.

Searching for Vic

In 1993, after he explained the circumstances of the night of the attack, Howard talked about the man who probably saved his life. He told me, "Vic Gorlinsky was also a captain at the time – a good officer and a good man, the kind you can depend on. They shot me clean through the upper jaw – second time it happened. I got shot in the same damned place during the Battle of the Bulge.

"I know full well, that were it not for Vic, I wouldn't have made it on the night of 8 July 1959, but Vic isn't the kind of guy that needs laurels and flowers thrown at his feet. We lost touch sometime ago, you know how that goes, but he lives in the D. C. area and you might be able to track him down."

Before the days of the Internet, I was unable to get in touch with Victor Gorlinsky, but based on leads that Howard had given me, I would eventually locate Vic, many years later in December 2011, when Vietnam veteran and historian Bruce Swander was successful in touching bases with Vic through Vic's youngest son Mark. From the first time I spoke to Howard until the first time I spoke to Vic, eighteen years had passed.

The foundation of much that is written in this book is based on the information Howard Boston shared with me and the finite details that Vic Gorlinsky filled in years later.

Every time we spoke, Howard would always ask, "Have you found Vic yet?" He once told me, "Vic's memory about the incident is probably better than mine, after all, for some of those mad minutes I was a little out of it. Vic will be the lynchpin who will bring the whole Buis/Ovnand Bien Hoa attack scenario into focus."

When I finally touched bases with Victor Gorlinsky, in his 88th year, his recollections of the facts coincided with Howard Boston's. I immediately realized that Vic's memory was still combat sharp.

Chapter 4
The Three Wars of Victor Gorlinsky

Captain Victor Gorlinsky, US Army
Bien Hoa, Vietnam 1959
LTC Victor Gorlinsky, US Army (ret.)

Victor Walter Gorlinsky has been instrumental in the undertaking to set the record straight on the 8 July 1959 attack at Bien Hoa. A retired Lieutenant Colonel living in Virginia, and a two tour Vietnam veteran, he was one of six men in the main building and mess hall at the BIF Compound when the opening credits to the Universal International movie, *The Tattered Dress,* starring Jeanne Crain and Jeff Chandler began. With his photographs of the compound and his memories of the events, both before and after the attack, and cross referenced with the recollections of Howard Boston, a three dimensional picture was brought into focus of all the pertinent events, as well as some of the trivia surrounding the incident.

Hungarian Heritage

Victor's father, Carl, was born on 27 October 1881, near the Polish border in Bohemia, part of the Austrian/Hungarian Empire, and as a young man worked in mines there. Victor's mother, Marie, was born on 14 April 1885, in Kutna Hora, Bohemia. Via different routes, the two young people made their way to America shortly after the turn of the Twentieth Century. Victor was born in Russellville, Arkansas, on 23 December 1923, the youngest of four Gorlinsky children.

Step-brothers Stanley and Carl Jr., Victor and his sister, Ellen, attended schools in Russellville. Victor dropped out of high school to join Headquarters Company, 153d Infantry, headquartered in his home town.

Arkansas Guard to Regular Army

"I enlisted on 2 April 1940 at the age of sixteen," said Vic. "It seemed like a good deal for me, since I was interested in amateur radio, and the fact that I made more money in one drill night with the National Guard than I made in a week delivering the *Arkansas Gazette* every day."

Originally known as the 1st Arkansas Volunteer Infantry during the Spanish-American War, the 153d Infantry was activated for World War I and shipped to France as part of the 39th Infantry Division, "Delta Division". Private Gorlinsky went to Minnesota for training and maneuvers in August 1940. He trained as a radio operator in the 3d Battalion's communications platoon, operating telephone and radio communications.

"That summer our regiment was sent to Minnesota for three weeks of maneuvers. Minnesota was very cold at night, but hot in the day time. The mosquitoes were big and there were thousands of them. We were fortunate to have campaign hats with broad brims – over these hats we wore head-nets to keep the mosquitoes away from our faces and necks. Putting up with the pests was a major chore, and a major accomplishment!"

"On 23 December 1940, my seventeenth birthday, the 153d was Federally Mobilized and called to active duty at Camp Joseph T. Robinson, near Little Rock," said Vic. "Two of us were sent to Fort Benning, Georgia, to attend the Infantry School's three-month radio operator's course."

In August 1941, the 153d Infantry participated in maneuvers at Shiloh National Park in Tennessee. "We contended with copperheads and water moccasins. This maneuver toughened us up pretty well. Our opposing force was a regular Army unit and we as National Guardsmen out-maneuvered them during that exercise.

"When we returned to Camp Robinson we didn't stay there long. The battalion that I operated the radio for was told to pack up and move out. By 1941, Europe was already in shambles with everything that Hitler was doing. We figured the big brass were getting ready to ship us overseas, and that we were headed for Europe. The United States was preparing for war. You can imagine our surprise when we were sent to the frozen mountains and tundra of Alaska.

"Our destination was Seward at the southern tip of the Kenai Peninsula. We arrived in mid-September 1941. Our unit's advanced party had gotten there before us and had erected pyramidal tents for us to live in. September was already cold that far north, especially at night, and the unit's tent city was heated by small individual conical shaped Sibly stoves. The first night was miserably cold and we quickly winterized our tents. Our first snow fell in October and we didn't see the end of snow until June of 1942. The Siblys burned wood at a furious rate, and for two winters our scrounging parties did a fairly good job of keeping the tents warm."

Vic Gorlinsky, and a small band of fellow soldiers, operated the base-camp radio station at Caines Head Outpost, fifteen miles northwest of Seward on Resurrection Bay, where a battery of San Francisco Coast Artillery manned 155mm Long Toms, providing defenses against enemy attack if the Japanese were to breach the bay.

"I was at Caines Head on December 7th, 1941, when the Japanese bombed Pearl Harbor. We didn't know if the Japs had any plans to do something in Alaska, and we were on a constant state of alert."

War in Europe

After Alaska Sergeant Gorlinsky was recommended for OCS and attended Class 26-43 at Fort Monmouth, New Jersey. During that time he was told to forget his enlisted rank and was addressed as "Candidate". The schooling lasted three months. Victor Gorlinsky was commissioned a second lieutenant in ceremonies on 10 August 1943. He was 19 years old.

In March 1944, Gorlinsky's group sailed for England on the *Aquatainia*, a British ship built around 1915. "We landed in Scotland and boarded trains for England. My destination was Cheltenham, near the west coast, where I was assigned to the 810th Signal Service Battalion.

"I was on duty in the communications center during the early morning hours on 6 June 1944, when the D-Day invasion took place. As it became daylight, I heard the noise of many airplanes overhead, and as I went outside I saw numerous troop carriers that had dropped paratroopers in Normandy. We could see that many of those aircraft coming back from France had been hit by flak, had holes in them, and missing parts of their wings and tail sections, as well as having other shell-fire damage. About 0800 hours [Greenwich Mean Time], radio stations began broadcasting General Eisenhower's message announcing that the invasion was in progress."

In November 1944, the 810th Signal Service Battalion was shipped across the English Channel to Le Havre, France, and traveled by motor transport to Paris.

"I didn't get to see any of the big parades down the Champs Elysees," said Vic. "Paris had been liberated for about two months by the time I got there."

When he got to Paris, Lieutenant Gorlinsky worked at 26 Avenue Klebier. Vic supplied and redistributed communications equipment

When Victor Gorlinsky arrived in Paris, the Champs Elysees bore little vehicular traffic, except for a few bicycles, occasional horse drawn carts and infrequent U.S. Army convoys. (Photo taken from atop a deuce-and-a-half) Author's collection

for a myriad of U.S. Army functions. "I made one trip to the Normandy beaches to help recover communications equipment and supplies," said Vic. "There was a lot of mud. It had been raining steadily and everything was damp, cold and wet.

"It was thought that the war was going to end soon and preparations were being made to occupy Germany. Belgium had also been liberated and Antwerp was going to be the port where our equipment would arrive.

"On 17 December 1944, we drove a 1 ½ ton telephone-line-truck from Paris to the Courcelles Signal Depot in Belgium. It was a sunny day and we stopped to heat our C-Rations on the engine block of the truck, oblivious to the fact that the Germans had launched the Ardennes Offensive – The Battle of the Bulge."

When Gorlinsky arrived at the signal depot, he was surprised to see the high level of alert that U.S. troops were on. A few days later, on Vic's 21st birthday, a lone German aircraft flew low into Courcelles firing rounds of 20mm ammunition, as it attempted to hit a near-by railroad yard.

What Vic had no idea of at the time was that during that same week Staff Sergeant Howard Boston, assigned to the 10th Armored Infantry Battalion, only miles away, was shot through the lower jaw during heavy fighting in the Ardennes Forest. Ironically, fourteen years later, in July 1959, in a place that was then still known as French Indochina, Victor Gorlinsky would save Boston's life, when Boston was again shot through the jaw - the second time between his upper teeth and his nose.

"The Battle of the Bulge ended when General George Patton's Third Army broke through the German lines relieving the 101st Airborne trapped at Bastogne. During the last days of that battle, the weather cleared enough for our airplanes to fly, and the sight of thousands of airplanes overhead was awe inspiring," Vic remembered. "I was in Belgium on VE Day, 8 May 1945. I stayed in Europe until September 1945, when I was sent back to the states."

Korea to Vietnam

After his discharge, Vic Gorlinsky went to college but after his adventures during World War II, he could not focus on studies and became restless. He returned to active duty in February 1948, but before he left, he married his sweetheart, Blanche, on 10 February, in Benton, Arkansas. During the Korean War, as a 1st Lieutenant, he served eighteen months in Korea, first with the 8229th Army Unit at Pusan and Tageau and, later, during heavy fighting near the 38th parallel, thirty-five miles east of Chun Chon with a radio intercept unit supporting the 2d and 7th infantry divisions.

"Vietnam was my next overseas assignment," said Vic. "I received orders in early 1959 to proceed there for duty with the Military Assistance Advisory Group Vietnam (MAAG). On arrival in Saigon, I learned that my actual duties would be as signal advisor with the Vietnamese 7th ARVN Infantry Division. There were a limited number of officers assigned to MAAG. My allocation was actually with TERM (Technical Equipment Recovery Mission), but my duties were with MAAG. It appeared to be a way of getting more advisors on the ground without violating the headcount agreement. Getting through the processing in Saigon took a few days. I had to get a Vietnamese driver's license, take refresher training with various weapons, and adjust to the time change. Finally, I arrived at the old French sawmill compound, affectionately called BIF for *Bureau Industrielle Forestier*. It was 8 May 1959 – exactly two months before the incident. There were several large buildings on the compound, one of which was used for billets and our mess hall. Some were used as quarters, while other smaller buildings were for the kitchen, power generator, and the cook's and guard quarters. The actual division compound was outside our gate and down the road about a mile.

Captain Victor Gorlinsky wears a "Fidel Castro" style M 1951 cotton field cap and bathing suit, as he travels the Dong Nai River in MAAG 7's power boat, "Miss America". LTC Victor Gorlinsky, US Army (ret.)

"We were in a well established routine which repeated itself each week," said Vic. "We trained the ARVN's five days and had Wednesday afternoons off, as well as Saturday afternoons, and all day Sunday. Sunday was our day for waterskiing. Some of us had extra duties. Mine happened to be taking care of the kitchen, collecting monies for the food we ate, preparing menus, buying food at the local Bien Hoa market place, or making Post Exchange runs to Saigon and handling the mail/distribution pick-up. These extra responsibilities kept me very busy so my time did pass without being bored."

Of all his experiences and his participation in two previous wars, the thing that sets Victor Gorlinsky's military career apart from all others, is that as of this writing, early 2012, he is the last surviving eyewitness to an important event in history. Not in Europe during World War II, nor during the Korean War, but as an eyewitness to the attack that occurred in Vietnam at Bien Hoa during the beginning of American involvement. Events that because of their significance have marked a granite monument in Washington, D. C. with the indelible date 1959.

Chapter 5
Hanging "Hanging Sam"

Lt General Samuel T. Williams, US Army
US Army photo

One might think that Lieutenant General "Hanging Sam" Williams, Commanding General of MAAG Vietnam, would have been one of the first officers on the scene after Major Buis, Captain Boston, and Master Sergeant Ovnand were gunned-down. However, Williams did not appear at the *Bureau Industrielle Forestier* (BIF) Compound at Bien Hoa until several days later. At the Oriental Hotel in Bangkok at the time of the attack, General Williams received information, initially funneled to him through the MAAG Vietnam duty officer, which as a brief summary of events, should not have been completely relied upon when it came to such a high profile incident without a thorough investigation.

The "Emergency" message dispatched by MAAG Staff Duty Officer Captain Robert H. Cushing, Jr., was addressed to Chief MAAG; CINCPAC Camp H. M. Smith, Territory of Hawaii; Department of the Army, Washington, DC.; and USARMA, Bangkok, Thailand.

"Confidential MAGAG-PO 659

1. Reference Conf MAGAG-CH 654.

2. Now verified two US Advisors killed and one US Advisor wounded in attack on 7th Inf Div Field Advisor Detachment at Bien Hoa. Killed were Major Dale R. Buis.., Infantry and Master Sergeant Chester M. Ovnand.., Wounded is Captain Howard B. Boston.., Artillery. Captain Boston suffered gunshot wound in head but not considered critical and will be evacuated Clarke [sp] Field, P.I., 9 July. Administrative reports on casualties have been submitted separately.

3. Details of attack are as follows:

a. At approximately 1900 hours local time 8 July estimated ten persons believed to be Viet Cong attacked US Advisory mess at Bien Hoa with small arms and one improvised bomb.
b. Attack occurred during showing of movie when lights were turned on to change reels. Six advisors were present.
c. Attackers apparently approached rear of area, traversed a fence, and then fired into building with small arms through five windows from positions immediately outside windows. One improvised bomb was thrown. Bomb hit screen and exploded outside building killing one attacker. One Advisor had physical contact outside building with one attacker.
d. In process of attack one Vietnamese soldier guard and one Vietnamese mess attendant were killed.
e. Duration of attack estimated to have been maximum of five minutes.
f. Vietnamese guard forces in area reacted quickly and drove off attackers.
g. Attack was single incident.

4. Appropriate additional security measures have been taken and AMEMB Saigon notified.

5. On Vietnamese side Chief of General Staff is making personal investigation, MAAG will send full report later.

6. No press release made to date. Any release made will be made by AMEMB Saigon.

7. COMSTOCK USARMA Saigon request DEPTAR pass to ACSI.

8. USARMA Bangkok pass to Lt. Gen William at Oriental Hotel."

Although General Williams immediately flew back to Saigon, he did not make an appearance at the scene of the attack until several days later. He depended on information he received from Colonel Charles Symroski, MAAG's intelligence officer, who had interviewed Victor Gorlinsky at the Brink Hotel on the night of the attack. Immediately after Colonel Symroski's briefing, William's primary concern appears to have been political, as the first thing he did was to confer with President Ngo Dinh Diem. When General Williams finally showed up at the BIF Compound a few days later, anyone who was familiar with him would not have been surprised at his cold reaction to the shootings.

"We had a number of U.S. and Vietnamese officials visit us after the attack, among them Lieutenant General Sam Williams," Victor Gorlinsky remembered. "He just sauntered around and pretty much played the part of an old grouch."

Although Captain Gorlinsky and others at the BIF compound were surprised at General Williams', seemingly, unfeeling demeanor, Williams was primarily concerned about the attack happening on "his watch". Anyone who knew about General Samuel "Hanging Sam" Williams' military career would have realized that the attack on Bien Hoa was not the first glitch during his tenure as a U.S. Army general.

Even as MAAG Commander when the 1959 attack occurred, General Williams' part in the incident, from an historical point of view, might have been far less significant if the only point was that he was MAAG commander then. However, when he was interviewed about the attack by an archivist at the Lyndon Baines Johnson Library, almost twenty-two years later, on 2 and 16 March 1981, and his statements were made public and part of the permanent record, it was realized that much of what he had to say did not coincide with the facts.

As I recognized that the general's statements about the attack must be addressed, I could devise no other way to dispute his statements without quoting him and addressing his military career.

Early Career

Samuel Tankersley Williams was born on 25 August 1897 in Denton, Texas. In May 1916 he enlisted in the Texas National Guard, and as a private, under the command of General John "Black Jack" Pershing, took part in the expedition into Mexico in search of Pancho Villa. In August 1917, Williams completed the officers training course at Camp Bullis, Texas, and was commissioned a second lieutenant in the U.S. Army Reserve Officers Corps.

During World War I, Sam Williams served with the 359th Infantry Regiment in France. He took part in the St. Mihiel and the Meuse-Argonne offensives in 1918. He was wounded twice, the second time seriously.

In 1920 Samuel Williams was commissioned a first lieutenant in the Regular Army. He went on to assignments with the 21st Infantry Regiment at Schofield Barracks, Hawaii, and the 29th Infantry Regiment at Fort Benning, Georgia. An accomplished polo player, he was a member of the U.S. Army's team which went on to capture an international championship. As he rose in position and rank, he graduated from both the Army Command and General Staff College in 1936, and the U.S. Army War College in 1938.

Demotion in Wartime

In 1942 Williams was promoted to brigadier general. In February 1943, he was appointed to the position of 90th Infantry Division's Assistant Division Commander. The 90th Division had a two year training period fraught with turmoil of resources and personnel. Therefore, the 90th Division went into World War II combat, on the shores of France, with numerous issues operating against it; as it contended with inexperienced cadre, unfamiliar doctrine, poor training in advanced combat skills, and the confusion and instability of constant personnel changes.

On 23 January 1944, less than five months before D-Day, artillery officer Brigadier General Jay W. MacKelvie assumed command of the 90th Division at Fort Dix, New Jersey. General MacKelvie seemed to have the credentials for command, however, according to an interview with Sam Williams, MacKelvie had his failings.

In a 26 April 1984 interview, General Williams stated that prior to his departure with the division's advanced party to England, he tried to ensure that General MacKelvie was properly briefed on all issues concerning the 90th Division, particularly on the status of troop replacements which Williams considered to be inadequate.

General Williams felt that the 90th Divisions' training also suffered in England between 10 April and 5 June 1944. The dividing of responsibilities between MacKelvie and Williams was never very clear and there were holes in their overlapping responsibilities.

General Williams, as the assistant division commander, normally oversaw daily training in preparation for combat, but he spent most of his time at XXII Corps Headquarters planning the 90th Division's tactical role in the invasion of Europe, and was not able to carry out his duties.

Between 6 and 10 June, as the 90th went ashore at Normandy's Utah Beach, infantrymen were forced to learn the lessons of training under fire and there were high casualty rates. The 90th Division's advance was severely slowed because the unit had not been trained in, nor had planned for, the difficulties of hedgerow combat.

After its bloody battle for Monte-Castre, the 90th Division was tasked to eradicate a salient obstacle centered in the town of St. Germaine. The result was disastrous for the division.

In his 1951 memoirs, General Omar Bradley criticized the 90th Infantry Division. Bradley stated that they were the worst trained division in the European Theater. All of this was a reflection on both MacKelvie and Williams. Major General Lawton Collins relieved General MacKelvie in July. The new division commander, Major General Eugene M. Landrum and Brigadier General Sam Williams became embroiled in a disagreement which developed into an altercation. On 14 July 1944, General Landrum stated, "I feel that a general officer of a more optimistic and calming attitude would be more beneficial to this division at this time." General Omar Bradley concurred and topped off Sam Williams' dismissal by demoting him to colonel. Sam Williams was reassigned to a staff position. He then planned missions in the European Theater of Operations, and despite previous problems he had with the 90th, he performed his new assignment well.

A Terrible Nickname

For many years, "Hanging Sam" Williams cut a notorious swatch in military legend. It was said he received his nickname because of his involvement at Nuremberg, during the Nuremberg War Trials, when eleven Nazi's were hung at Spangdahlem Prison.

A small group of allied military officers and eight newspaper men witnessed the event. It is not certain if Sam Williams was actually there, although innuendos such as "Hanging Sam Williams – You know – Nuremberg," seemed to be everywhere.

Sam Williams actually received his moniker when, as a member of a general court-martial in 1944, a soldier was tried for the rape and murder of a little girl. An endless parade of psychiatrists testified as to the man's lack of sanity. Williams lost his patience and exclaimed, "I've heard enough! Let's hang the son-of-a-bitch!" In

February 1946, when Williams took command of the 26th Infantry at Nuremberg, Germany, he revived his dormant nickname for the sake of striking fear and respect into the hearts of the soldiers of his new regiment.

"The news got out," said Williams in 1981, "and people started calling me 'Hanging Sam' - terrible nickname! But, by God, it's been in the army for an awful long time and to some a name of endearment. Now a lot of people thought it was because I was at Nuremburg and had the Nuremburg Fourth Enclave at the time of the execution of the war crime criminals, but I had that name long before I was at Nuremburg."

Colonel Williams was again promoted to Brigadier General in 1951. He gained another star in 1952. In 1955 he gained still another star when promoted to lieutenant general. Certainly, to be busted from brigadier general to colonel and, then, on sheer military merit rise to three-star-general is an incredible accomplishment.

Commander MAAG Vietnam

On 1 November 1955, General Williams was assigned as commander of the Military Assistance Advisory Group (MAAG) Vietnam in Saigon. He was the first officer assigned to the position, because former MAAG commanders in Vietnam had commanded MAAG Indochina, but since a separate advisory group had been established for Cambodia in June 1955, Williams' group dropped 'Indochina' from its name.

The 1959 attack on Bien Hoa was not the first enemy action under General Williams' tenure as MAAG Vietnam commander. U.S. military personnel had suffered their first casualties when thirteen Americans (3 officers, 6 soldiers and 4 civilians) were wounded in three terrorist bombings occurring in Saigon on 22 October 1957; an explosive device hurled under a military bus at the Metropole Hotel, a smaller bomb lodged in a large flower plot at a MAAG Cholon officers billet, and an explosion occurring at the U.S. Information Service Library. The military severely wounded in those attacks were: Major John Cevaal, Major Elsworth Reiss, Captain

On 22 October 1957, two bombs, intended to kill Americans, were planted near the MAAG Headquarters in Saigon. US Army photo

The U.S. Information Services Abraham Lincoln Library was the target of the other bombing on 22 October 1957. Author's collection

David C. Womack, M/Sgt Frank E. Kent, M/Sgt Charles E. Kille, M/Sgt Charles G. McQuay, SFC Charles G. Grant, SP4 Donald A. Ruths and SP3 Theodoria Rosario-Mendez. The other four wounded in the bombings were U.S. civilians, while U.S. Army Special Forces Captain Harry G. Cramer, Jr., had been killed in a mysterious explosion at Nha Trang, seventy-five miles to the northwest, during a training exercise the day before (see also page 165).

Captain Harry G. Cramer, Jr., US Army
Courtesy of LTC Hank Cramer, US Army (ret.)

In General Williams' 183 page biography, *HANGING SAM,* written by Colonel Harold J. Meyer, U.S. Army (ret.), there is no mention of the three 1957 bombings, the explosion at Nha Trang, or the attack on Bien Hoa, which took the lives of Major Buis and M/Sgt Ovnand, although "Chapter 11 Vietnam: 1955-1960" is a prominent chapter in the book. On page 141, General Williams is quoted as describing the situation in Vietnam, which began in 1957, saying:

> "I began to gather information that the hard-core communists were coming down, and incidents of murder and casualties in the simple farm villages began to happen with a country-wide frequency. These communists were coming from the north and would contact a member of the Viet Cong who was planted in a village a couple of years earlier. From him, they would find out the names of the peasants loyal to Diem and

> the army. Come sunrise, the local loyals and their wives and children would be found murdered with their bodies violated in the worst possible manner and strewn in the dirt road. Terrible. Simple peasants uprising? No, the perpetrators of such cowardly acts were soldiers of the north, and they were assisted in these deeds by their planted communist agents."

In his 2 and 16 March 1981 interviews with an archivist at the Lyndon Baines Johnson Library, General Williams did not give the 22 October 1957 bombings even a cursory mention, and at the age of eighty-four, he advanced a distorted view of the events that happened on 8 July 1959 at Bien Hoa.

Memory Lapse and Balderdash

"I know one of the first times we had casualties there, it was out at Bien Hoa if I remember correctly," said General Williams, who had been retired for some 21 years, since 31 August 1960. "It was after supper and the Americans were in their dining room and they put up a little motion picture machine and were looking at motion pictures. Suddenly some people appeared in the windows, local Vietnamese were already at the windows looking in, kids and people there at that post looking through the windows at the picture show. Some of these outlaws appeared and sprayed inside the room with automatic weapons. One of them appeared to throw a bomb or a grenade of some kind through a kitchen door. He was countered in that, because there were two screen doors about ten feet apart. He apparently didn't know about the second screen door, and so the thing bounced back on him and they found his remains outside the next morning.

"I happened to be in Bangkok that particular day that it happened, but I got a message of this attack. I got over there as fast as an airplane could take me. I told Diem, 'This is no good. I don't know what our casualties are. There's three or four people wounded and I think one or two dead.'" Then to emphasize the context of the interview, "...but I'm not positive and it makes no difference now at this late date. Lord take care of their souls."

Sam continued, "I said, '...This case must be solved.' Later Landsdale [*] told me, 'The Vietnamese thought so much about this that they broke some of their security finding-out who did this.' So those people, the best I could find up until now, came three days marches from the north. In other words, they left someplace in the north, and I never did know the details and I didn't particularly care to, if I had known I couldn't have remembered anyway.

"They left a particular place in the north and they walked all night. Then they went into hiding during the day. Another guide picked them up. They were strangers, they didn't know the country. Another guide would pick them up, walked them all night. So for three nights they walked. They got to this place and then they botched their job, because the windows were too high so they couldn't shoot down at the seats."

There is much rebuttal concerning General Williams' statements.

The general stated that one of the attackers attempted to throw an explosive device through the kitchen door, but because there were two screen doors ten feet apart, the charge bounced back killing him. The only screen doors which were ten feet apart was the one into the separate kitchen building, and the other at the main building which led to the kitchen via the causeway. This, in itself, had no relevance when the Viet Cong sapper attempted to launch his explosives. He was standing between the two doors. There was, by all photographic evidence, a set of outside shutters on the main building kitchen door, similar to the shutters on the main building windows, while both the kitchen screen door and the door in the main building leading to the kitchen, opened both inward and outward depending which way one pushed. With the shutters open, as they were, there would not have been anything to prevent the screen door from being pushed open inwardly by the momentum of the satchel charge being thrown... But, there was! General Williams, had no idea the obstruction was Major Buis who prevented the satchel charge from being thrown into the main building.

* U.S. Air Force Colonel Edward G. Landsdale headed the Saigon Military Mission which was a special CIA team.

Secondly, even if the infiltrators force-marched at near superhuman effort in three nights, they may have been able to get from the Cambodian border to Bien Hoa, but certainly not from North Vietnam. Thus, they did "come from the north" but not immediately from North Vietnam in three days as Williams' suggested.

More on the STEN

Captain Victor Gorlinsky was six feet tall. The windows at the mess hall, via photographic evidence, came approximately to his waist or about three feet from the ground, therefore, the attackers had plenty of room to see over the window sills. This was a second incorrect assumption made on the part of General Williams. The bullet round marks, high on the walls, had nothing to do with the height of the windows. The communist attackers had used a STEN machinegun, an English-manufactured 32 round blowback action magazine fed weapon. The magazine stuck out to the user's left (bolt fixed). It was a wild gun which was hard to control because of the weight of the bolt and its impact. When manufactured, the STEN was pressed out and welded together and relatively simple to

fabricate, like the more commonly familiar M1A1 grease gun. British soldiers were trained to hold down on the STEN so that its firing path would not rise up, higher and higher, as it was fired. It is, pretty much, certain that the VC attackers were not properly trained to fire the STEN. The STEN was the British answer to the MP40 German 9mm grease gun which also had a forceful rise to it. STENs fired a solid jacketed round designed to go through a soldier and wound him in combat rather than kill outright. The full metal jacket rounds were in concurrence with the Geneva accords. During World War II, the French underground easily fabricated STEN machine guns and once made were readily issued to their clandestine troops, thus, their availability. It is apparent that Lieutenant General Sam Williams recalled being told that some of the 9mm rounds had hit high on the mess hall interior wall, and he needed his own explanation as to why some of the firing had been so erratic. It was not because the windows were too high, but because a STEN machinegun, rather than a MAT-49, was used in the communist's attempt to wipe out the American advisors, and STENs were extremely difficult to control.

More Rebuttal

General Williams also stated, "The people that were hurt were trying to get their weapons. By that time I'd told our people to always keep a weapon handy. Now, we weren't supposed to be armed. But I never went anyplace that I didn't have a .45. I said, 'You can carry weapons without advertising it to the world, not even your Vietnamese compadre needs to know that you're carrying a .45. But for Christ's sake, carry something!' These advisors weren't carrying them because they were sitting in their own dining room they'd left their damn weapons upstairs. That's stupid. The reason some people don't survive is because they do things like that. But anyway, the people that were shot were going up the staircase."

What is blatantly offensive here is that as MAAG Vietnam Commander, it was General Sam Williams who issued the directive, telling MAAG advisors they were specifically *not* authorized to carry weapons of any kind under any circumstances. Victor Gorlinsky distinctly recalls, "We were not allowed to carry fire arms or even have any in our quarters. Major Beau Turner had a shot gun which was in direct violation of MAAG Vietnam policy and directives."

Gorlinsky's recollections about the MAAG policy of not being allowed to carry firearms was reinforced in a letter written by Major Dale Buis to his wife, Virginia, shortly before his death, in which he explained that in Vietnam "the situation was getting out of hand" but MAAG "was not issuing weapons because we are not here to fight - just advise."

"After the July 1959 attack, we ignored the MAAG ruling, which was still in place, and obtained a number of weapons and hand grenades we kept near us at all times," said Gorlinsky. "Since I traveled to Saigon two or three times a week, after the attack I carried my loaded .45 caliber pistol in a hand bag…but that was *after* the attack!"

Maybe it was assumed by General Williams that Master Sergeant Ovnand was trying to get to the only weapon the MAAG advisors had available to them, which was an unauthorized personal shot gun owned by Captain Beau Turner. That was not the case, although it simplified General Williams' explanation of what happened. In January 2012 Victor Gorlinsky stated, "One thing for sure, Captain Turner's shotgun was not on the second floor of the main building. Turner and I had quarters in a different building, located just to the right of the entry way, off the main road. Beau Turner's shotgun was in those quarters. Master Sergeant Ovnand climbed the stairs for one reason, and one reason only – to turn on the outside flood lights to break the attack."

Contrary to General Williams' interview, no one in MAAG 7 had .45 caliber pistols. Weapons were not authorized, none were issued, and none had been shipped clandestinely by members of the unit to Vietnam. Further, no directives, either written or verbal, had been passed down stating that MAAG personnel should be secretly carrying .45 semi-automatics. Howard Boston commented, "Even after the attack, if General Williams had known that advisors at MAAG 7 were carrying personal fire arms, he would have probably hung the offenders!"

Hanging Sam continued, "The raiders killed a Vietnamese girl that lived there. She happened to be standing outside on a box, or something, watching the movie…They didn't give a damn who they killed."

No little girl was killed during the firing, or the explosion. The mess cook's eight year old son was hit by three bullets in the chest. Howard Boston distinctly remembered, "He was hit by gun fire and was being treated next to me by the Vietnamese medics." General Williams either had faulty memory on this subject, had never really been clear on what had happened, or was attempting to dramatize the attack which he may have felt seemed more gripping and more atrocious that a little Vietnamese girl was killed, rather than a little Vietnamese boy was hit in the chest by three 9mm rounds and suffered an unknown fate. His "standing on a box, or something" comment was part of his inventiveness, otherwise, how could a "little girl" be able to see the movie through a window, when the Viet Cong could not see into the building through windows of the same height?

Speaking about the Viet Cong, General Williams explained that, "[They found] the remains of one of them there. He had been killed by his own grenade. But that was the only hard evidence that I recall that someone had come down from the north. But, of course, I knew, or at least I believed, that these people were coming down and they would go to these places and they would intimidate these villagers and they would make certain recruits."

The original message sent to General Williams while he was staying at the Oriental Hotel in Bangkok stated, "One advisor had physical contact outside the building with one attacker." It is interesting that General Williams gave no credit to one of his MAAG military advisors for stopping the sapper at the door from throwing the satchel charge in the mess hall. Either he had never investigated what had happened, or he had forgotten those details.

General Samuel T. Williams was described by one of his contemporaries as an "old army officer – disciplined, confident, loyal, and strong." He was a cantankerous individual, self career minded, and although fearless in battle, after he arrived in South Vietnam on 28 October 1955, he became very political in character and saw his role as one of "army building". General Williams retired from the United States Army on 31 August 1960. He died on 26 April 1984.

It is apparent that General Williams, had he known all the facts about the 8 July 1959 attack on the MAAG Compound at Bien Hoa, by his 2 and 16 March 1981 interviews had forgotten much, had distorted much, and had numerous false recollections about the incident. It appears he was filling in the blanks, with any answer that came to mind, as he went along with the interview. His comments on the attack at Bien Hoa are part of the permanent record at the National Archives and Records Service at the Lyndon Baines Johnson Library, and needed antidote and corrections to his distortions concerning those events which are on record there. Many of his comments about the advisors who died that night were incorrect, offensive and inappropriate.

Chapter 6
Major Dale R. Buis

Dale R. Buis, US Army
Korean War-era photo
Photo courtesy of Buis family

Dale Richard Buis, son of Dr. Jon and Serena Buis, was born in Pender, Nebraska, on 29 August 1921. He grew up with his sisters, Elizabeth and Margaret, and brothers Harold and James.

Gertrude Essex Knudson, a Pender, Nebraska, school teacher, remembered Buis quite well, "Dale was eight or nine years old when he came to my class for the first time. He was a happy, healthy boy, rather tow headed with beautiful brown eyes. He enjoyed school and had zest for everything."

Dale's nephew, Hon. J. Stephen Buis, was told, "From an early age, Dale was known for his pranks. While in high school he led a cow into the school house, but as if that were not enough, he led it up the stairs into the bell tower. I can't imagine the reaction of students and teachers when they heard the mooing above them in the school belfry."

Wentworth Military Academy

"Dale went to Wentworth Military Academy in Lexington, Missouri, where he played football," said Stephen. "My father [Dale's brother], who also once played, said that Dale played a 'different game' than he had. Dale was hardnosed and tough. He didn't let anything get by him and always charged right for the ball."

"While Dale was at Wentworth several attempts were made, by recruiters, to get him to play football for various schools," said Stephen. "One of which was North Carolina, however, Dale decided to pursue the military once the war broke out."

Another person that remembered Dale as a young athlete and cadet, was Don Durham, "As cadets at Wentworth, Dale and I were close. He was the cadet company commander of Company A. I was only a buck sergeant, but because I was older he'd sometimes look to me for guidance. Dale possessed some very fine qualities. He was a leader and quite a guy. He was six foot, or maybe six foot one, muscular, and played football on the academy teams. I remember that he had reddish-blonde hair and his ears stuck out a little bit.

"We were in our last year in Wentworth when we got word that the Japs had bombed Pearl Harbor. He and I went to Frank Brown, the commandant, and told him we were going to Kansas City to enlist in the Army Air Corps to fight Japs. We were determined to join, but we also expected him to tell us we couldn't. Surprisingly, Commandant Brown wished us luck. We hitchhiked to Kansas City where we took the aviation cadet test at the induction center. We went back to Wentworth awaiting the results, but were never informed of the outcome of the tests. I guess, Commandant Brown had called and told them that we only had a short time to go before we would be commissioned as infantry officers. After we went on active duty, Dale went his way, and I went mine."

Dale Buis entered the U.S. Army on 1 July 1942. As a second lieutenant, he was first stationed at Camp Forrest, Tennessee, with the 136th Infantry. After several training transfers, the 136th arrived in Hawaii on 15 July 1943, and after more training departed the

Dale Buis sits on the steps of a military billet wearing a service cap folded to his liking. Photographs courtesy of Hon. J. Stephen Buis

A class leader at Wentworth - three strips up and two down, Dale Buis' rank insignia bore a diamond center.

"I still relish listening to the cheers from the stands while playing football, baseball and basketball," Dale Buis wrote from Vietnam.

Dale Buis was an accomplished javelin thrower while attending Wentworth Military Academy.

islands on 30 April 1944, arriving at Finschhafen, New Guinea, on 11 May 1944. Shortly after his arrival on New Guinea, Buis was transferred to the 27th Infantry Division, headed for Saipan.

Fighting in the Pacific

Stephen Buis recalled, "Although Dale only spoke of his wartime experiences once, I know he fought in the Pacific during World War II. He visited Richmond several times in 1957 and 1958, when I was 14 and 15. One of those times we were sitting on my parent's patio, when a *Victory at Sea* episode came on the television, and he mentioned, very matter of fact, that he had fought on the Island of Saipan. He said, 'Yeah, the 27th had to come in and straighten things out for the Marines.'"

On 15 June 1944, the Second and Fourth Marine divisions invaded Saipan, then the following day, the U.S. Army's 27th Infantry Division, under the command of General Ralph C. Smith, arrived on the beaches between the two Marine divisions. Marine Corps General Holland "Howlin' Mad" Smith, relieved General R. C. Smith on the second day of the 27th's participation in the attack, because of the slow progress being made by the 27th in the valley they were ordered to advance through. According to Robert J. Sloan of the 27th's G2 section, there was a thick cloud cover and aerial reconnaissance was useless. The valley was surrounded by hills and cliffs that the Japanese controlled. Yet, under a plan developed by General Ralph C. Smith, which was implemented after he was relieved, one battalion of the 27th Division held the area, while two other battalions flanked the Japanese successfully. Dale Buis played a part in the mission – a mission finally accomplished.

Although Dale never told Stephen what had happened once his unit got ashore, he did tell him, "Before we hit the beach, they issued me a twelve gauge shotgun and when I stepped off the landing craft into the water the Japs were right there to meet us swinging Samurai Swords. Waist deep in water, I just began shooting Japs faster than they realized what was happening."

"That image of Dale stuck with me all these years," said Stephen.

(Left) A shot gun was always Dale Buis' firearm of choice (Right) While on New Guinea, prior to combat on Saipan, Dale Buis stands in his utility uniform wearing a standard campaign hat. Photos courtesy of Hon. J. Stephen Buis

Occupation of Japan

After the atomic bombs were dropped on Hiroshima and Nagasaki, Japan offered its unconditional surrender. The formal ceremonies occurred aboard the USS *Missouri* on 2 September 1945. The United States occupation of Japan was one of the two major military governances, along with South Korea given to the U.S. Army at the close of the war. Unlike the set up in Germany, the Japanese government, under the guidance of General Douglas MacArthur, was delegated to administer the day to day operation of the country. General Headquarters (GHQ) worked on the "4 D's" - demilitarization, disarmament, democratization and deconcentration of the Japanese Zaibatzu (the industrial and financial conglomerates of family controlled monopolies whose influence allowed for control over significant parts of the Japanese economy). MacArthur established GHQ on the sixth floor of the Dai-Ichi Life Insurance building in downtown Tokyo, after GHQ was briefly based in Yokohama. By 1947, one of the staff sections under the Supreme Commander included "Civil Intelligence" to which Dale Buis was assigned. Buis had arrived in Japan immediately after the occupation began.

General Headquarters GHQ was on the sixth floor of the Dai-Ichi Life Insurance building in downtown Tokyo where Dale and Virginia worked. Author's collection

Good Times at the Yuraku

Japan was where Dale met his wife Virginia. "...Dale and I both worked at GHQ in Military Intelligence G-2 in Tokyo, where I was the administrative assistant to General Eric H. F. Svensson," said Virginia. "Dale and I would have many discussions far into the evening. There was sort of kinship in our thinking, and in our own form of humor.

"Although we worked like the devil through the day, and put in many hours after 5 P.M. It was a ritual to meet in the Yuraku Officers' Club – We had a group we called the 'Five O' Clock Club' that had about ten members – all bachelor officers. Charlie-San, the bar tender, had glasses with everyone's name on them. They made me an 'honorary member'.

"About 6:30 P.M. a jeep would rush me back to my quarters to clean up for the night, and then Dale would appear at about 8 bells with an orchid in hand.

"We had some very pleasant memories," said Giny. "On that first Japan tour, Hurema, the leader of the Japanese band, played every night at the Yuraku Officers' Club. He would play our song, *Love Letters*, every time Dale and I came into the club... He would just stop playing whatever song he was playing at the time, and go right into *Love Letters*..., and we would begin our evening of fun and games. We had two very enjoyable years in Tokyo.

Lieutenant Dale Buis wears a 27th Infantry Division shoulder insignia, while he and his future wife, Virginia, sit at the bar at the Yuraku BOQ in Tokyo. Courtesy of Hon. J. Stephen Buis

"Dale and I would stroll in Hibya Park; go to the Ernie Pyle Theatre every Sunday evening and then hurry back to the Yuraku Bar for fear of missing something.

"On the weekends, we'd go to the skeet range and once I out-shot Dale. My victory went all over the grape vine. Major General William F. Marquat, who was on General MacArthur's staff, was with us that day, and from then on, whenever he would spot me.., out would come his roar 'Hello Annie Oakley.'"

The Ernie Pyle Theatre in downtown Tokyo, Japan, was named for the famous war correspondent, killed, 18 April 1945, on Ie Shima (Ie Jima Island), northwest of Okinawa. Author's collection

During Sunday-off-duty-time, while crow hunting, Buis fell into a "honey-pit," and as if being covered with human waste was not enough, he scraped his leg on the sharp edge of the pit. The story had everyone laughing and got all the way to the top. In those days, the top was none other than General Douglas MacArthur, who according to feed-back, had a good chuckle over the incident.

Dale was hospitalized, received a tetanus shot, released to his quarters and told not to stand or walk on it. As a joke, Giny went down to Tokyo's Ginza buying lots of mechanical toys and strong smelling flowers. She then went to Dale's quarters, where she placed the flowers just out of his reach, wound up all the toys, placed them on the floor to hop, bounce, whirl, and spin around, then simply left!

"He was absolutely raving about the smelly flowers and the mechanical toys that he couldn't reach to stop when we met several days later!" Giny said. "Dale was a lot of fun – had a wonderful sense of humor, and we laughed a lot about nothing."

"I think we would have been content to just have gone on like that without any real commitment. Neither one of us really considered marriage, but that's what happened. We were married in a simple ceremony, and we were absolutely enthralled when our first son, Kurt, was born."

Pakistan Peace Keeping Force & Korea

During the good times in Japan in 1947 and 1948, a war between India and Pakistan raged in the Middle East, over Jammu and the Princely State of Kashmir. When a formal cease fire was declared at midnight, 1 January 1949, neutral military observers were needed. Retired U.S. Air Force Colonel William E. Naylor remembered, "Dale was my roommate at the Yuraku Hotel in Tokyo in 1948 and 1949. He was always seeking action and adventure. We both volunteered as U.S. military observers to Kashmir in 1949, but Dale developed a severe leg infection in Pakistan and had to return to Japan for treatment."

Buis' leg was still acting up because of the micro-organisms present in human "night-soil" which was used on fields and gardens in Japan. After his evacuation from Pakistan and treatment at Camp Zama, his leg healed without further complications and he was again fit for duty as the Korean War beckoned.

After Korea, Buis returned to Japan where he was stationed at Camp Younghans at Sendai. He was awarded an Army Commendation Medal for distinguished service while working with Eighth Army Intelligence.

Second Japan Tour to Fort Benning

"After the Korean War on our second Japan tour, I joined the 'Society of Hokkaido Widows,'" wrote Giny Buis, "Hokkaido being the northern island's bivouac area for the members of G-2 of the IX Corps...the many bivouacs that ensued during our two years at Sendai seemed strange when you consider that the other groups G-1, G-3 and G-4 made very few trips up there. Of course, Colonel Perlett was the G-2, and Dale and his cohorts were not above dreaming up various field trips for any number of reasons."

What Virginia Buis was not cognizant of, was the fact that Camp Chitose on the northern tip of the island of Hokkaido was less than 30 miles across the La Perouse Strait, facing the Soviet Union's Sakhalin Island, and therefore, IX Corps, G-2 Military Intelligence personnel had business at the location where the Army Security Agency had a semi-permanent camp. G2 was watching the Soviets, watching Chitose, watching the Soviets.

"Dale got his promotion to major before we left for the States in August 1955," said Giny.

After Japan, Major Buis and his family were transferred to Fort Benning, Georgia.

"Dale's assignment to Fort Benning with G-4 was a real blow to him, and he never got over the change in his status from an intelligence officer in G-2 to a logistics officer. We couldn't get quarters right away and the motel room got awfully small. From intelligence to logistics...and all the other aggravation of stateside duty, the idea was to get out of Fort Benning."

"He felt that it was the duty of all people to keep communism from our shores, although he often remarked that until bombs drop on the ole U.S.A. many people would be apathetic about the military-reasoning to intervene in some far-off foreign land that most of them had never heard of – much less could spell correctly!"

"When Dale requested a short overseas tour, I came back to California and, of course, he came with me to get me settled in."

Chief Warrant Officer 4 Mitsugi Kasai remembers Dale's time in California. He was one of his instructors at the U.S. Army Language School at Monterey. It was early 1958, and Dale was taking language lessons for Vietnamese before his deployment to Southeast Asia. "I know he had spent a total of two-and-a-half years in combat in two wars. He had five six-month hash marks on his sleeve," said CW4 Kasai. "Dale was a very conscientious student, a good friend, and based on his personality, military bearing, and military knowledge, one of the finest soldiers I have ever served with. I was shocked and saddened when I read about him a year later in the newspapers."

A Letter from Vietnam

Buis was granted assignment to MAAG Vietnam. He flew on military transport from Travis Air Force Base to Tan Son Nhut after several stops in the Pacific. Upon his arrival he reported to MAAG Saigon, where he was interviewed by Colonel Nathaniel P. Ward III, and received his assignment to Advisory Team 5.

Major Buis had already been at Song Mao, Binh Thuan Province for several months, when he wrote a letter on Monday morning, 27 April 1959. He made multiple copies using carbon paper. The letter was not addressed to anyone specifically, but rather he, jokingly, addressed it to "Peepul". One copy was sent to his brother Dr. L. James Buis, M.D.

"In that this is a Vietnamese type-writer the keyboard is quite a bit different than an American machine – 'tis several months since I have attempted to use one of these things – It's held together by string and rubber bands. I make no promises as to just what will appear on this or the following pages. Believe you will agree that it is a bit disconcerting to attempt to hit a period and end up with a semi-colon. Oh well, this is a 'hardship tour'. . .

Major Dale Buis arrived in Song Mao in November 1958. Here, at his unit of assignment, he stands at a sign which reads, *MAAG DETACHMENT, 5TH INFANTRY DIVISION, MAAG VIETNAM, SU DOAN BU BINH,* bearing both the early MAAG insignia, and the early insignia of the 5th ARVN Infantry Division. Photo courtesy of Gretchen Buis

"News from here is deadly boring: All the regiments and part of the special troops are on a 'security mission' and have been gone from here since the first part of this month. This mission consists of our Vietnamese troops going to different areas where rebel groups are in operation and said rebels are, of course, done away with. In that it is the rule that small fire-fights usually happen, U.S. Advisors are not allowed to accompany their units so for the next three to five months I will sit here at Song Mao doing absolutely nothing. For the time being, my days consist of sitting, reading, sleeping, painting and playing tennis. Sounds nice, but a steady diet of this nature soon grows most weary.

"The night before my unit departed – the regimental commander gave a farewell dinner – I was the only American advisor invited. Sitting down to the table, my interpreter looked at one particular food course and promptly informed me that he would not partake of it. He would not tell me what it consisted of. The CO of the Regimental heavy weapons company picked up this dish, telling me it was the favorite dish of the Vietnamese and I must try it. This, of course, put me behind the eight-ball and to save face I spooned a couple of spoons-full onto my plate. It was a jelly type food and had what appeared to be meat mixed in with the jelly. After a couple of bites, I told my interpreter that this tasted like 'blood-pudding' found on the plains of the mid-west. Much too his surprise I was right, but still I cannot state from any authority that the national dish of Vietnam is a mixture of coagulated blood and raw monkey brains.

"The dry season has finally come to an end – rainy season has begun and I wish that the dry season was back again. It is true that we no longer have to cope with our 20 to 30 knot winds and the swirling clouds of dust, but we no longer have even a semblance of a breeze and the humidity is constantly in the high 90's. At night when I go to sleep, I keep a towel by the bed so that at intervals during the night I can wipe the sweat off me and out of my eyes. The sting of sweat in your eyes will wake you as fast, if not faster, than a glass of cold water thrown in your face. In addition to the humidity caused by the rains – we are presently plagued with flying ants, frogs and very large lizards. It seems that the rain has washed all the flying ants and termites out of their holes – our evening meal usually consists of meat with fried or roasted ants; vegetables with ants, gravy with ants and so on. The frogs have come out after the ants and the large lizards are out after the frogs. The natives are most happy the rainy season is here as they once again have plenty of water, plus the fact they consider the lizards a delicacy dish. The lizards, by the way, are about three foot long and, I must admit, the tails are white meat and very tasty. You might say they are 'chicken with a slither'?

"I went to Saigon three weeks ago with the other two regimental advisors on a three day pass. This was the first time in over five months that I had been away from Song Mao. Spent a Tuesday and a Wednesday looking around and Thursday I spent in bed recovering from what I thought to be a king-sized hangover. This was not so! We did have quite a time just walking up and down streets, looking in the various shops and being treated like 'country bumpkins' by the people at MAAG Headquarters. I found that prices on curios and antiques are sky-high and any thoughts I had of obtaining loot from out here rapidly disappeared. We did join various 'bird watching clubs' in Saigon, which is nothing more than sitting in the sidewalk cafes and watching the gals go up and down the street. I must admit I find 'round eyes' much more attractive than any of the local 'belles'.

"I got back to Song Mao on a Friday morning and what I thought was a king-size hangover did not end. I stayed in bed over the weekend and finally caught the milk-run airplane back to Saigon on Tuesday. I went to the American dispensary and after many days of tests they found I have an infection in my right kidney. I had several X-Rays taken and they have been sent to Clark Field, Philippines, for further evaluation. Seems as how I have either a kink in the right tube or else a stone has been lodged there. I was put on antibiotics to do away with the infection, but tests still proved a bit of an infection remained the last time I was tested. Spent a week in Saigon and came back to Song Mao on the usual weekly milk-run. At present, I'm just sitting around waiting for the final X-Ray results to come back from Clark Field to see what's what. I don't feel too good and have some discomfort in my back. I have to write to the doctor tomorrow to see if the results have returned, and if so – what will be done.

"I received the magazines and books sent from the States while I was laying around in Saigon getting checked out at the dispensary. They couldn't have arrived at a better time as there was nothing to do until they arrived. Unfortunately, I am not a 'who-dun-it' fan, but the rest of the people here in the detachment are all reading the books. I find my tastes still run to westerns and historical novels, again, my thanks and the thanks of the people here in the detachment."

Among the books and magazines was a 1958 copy of *Dell Sports Baseball Stars* magazine with Ted Williams on the front cover, so Dale continued with, "Also my thanks for the baseball magazine. I must admit that Ted Williams has always been my favorite.

"I very emphatically find that tennis and golf are by no means a sissy game, and the doubles we play here get down right dangerous. We find it fair game to charge the net and reach over it while playing doubles and if anyone is silly enough to get in the way of your racket – it's their hard luck! I wish I had taken up both tennis and golf several years ago, although I still relish listening to the cheers from the stands while playing football, baseball and basketball of years long gone by...

"Although there is much hunting to be had here in Vietnam, it is all big game stuff and I find I get more enjoyment making a good shot on a dove than knocking down the four footed big game out here. I patiently wait for the time when I can get out of the army, settle down someplace and be able to take the kids on a hunting trip!

"I presently plan on spending about a week back in Omaha in early December of this year, once my tour here is up. I have already made my travel arrangements back to the 'Zone of the Interior' and will depart from Vietnam on 10 November 1959. I will take a 45 day leave, and after Thanksgiving will head back to Nebraska and get in a couple days of pheasant hunting and get some sitting around gabbing in.

"Seems to be all – have written far too much as it is. I am still looking forward to a hunting, or fishing trip sometime in the far future. For now –

"Same,

"Dale"

Insight

Dale Buis' 22 April 1959 letter is insightful because it indicates five significant facts: (1) Only through his letter do we know that at the time MAAG 5 was located at Song Mao in Binh Thuan Province, 67 miles southwest of Phan Rang in the Central Highlands. It was a distance of 135 road miles from Bien Hoa; (2) we also know that in 1959, U.S. advisors were not allowed to go into the field on combat operations with the units they were advising; (3) the unit that Dale Buis was advising would be gone from Song Mao on operation for, at least, the months of May, June and July, and possibly as long as through September; (4) we learn that Major Buis had kidney complications that required he make trips to the U.S. Army Dispensary in Saigon which was the reason he ended up in Bien Hoa on the night of 8 July 1959; and (5) we know conclusively that Dale Buis had not just arrived in Vietnam days earlier as press reports claimed. He had been in Vietnam since November 1958.

Chapter 7
Master Sergeant Chester M. Ovnand

M/Sgt Chester M. Ovnand, US Army, during World War II
Photo courtesy of Ovnand family

Chester Melvin Ovnand was born in Thief River Falls, Minnesota, on 8 September 1914, to Engebert and Maybell Ovnand. As a teenager, known by friends as "Chet," he lived with his mother in Excelsior, Minnesota. He quit high school in 1929, to help her financially. By the time Chet was twenty-eight, he was married to his first wife Catherine Irene Reynard. The couple had a daughter, Margaret Ann. They divorced at the time of their daughter's 5th birthday. Chet had a well paying job in Wisconsin when on 3 June 1942, he was inducted into the U.S. Army. Striving for military achievement, Chet Ovnand applied for Officer's Candidate School at Fort Knox, Kentucky, and was assigned to the 9th OCS Company. He graduated in April 1943, and was commissioned in the Armored Corps, assigned to a tank battalion.

Deployed to the Pacific

Lieutenant Ovnand was deployed to the Pacific Theater with the 1st Cavalry Division in late 1943. In January 1944 the 1st Cavalry Division established its command post at Cap Sudets, New Guinea, and during February and March 1944 was involved in heavy fighting on Los Negros and Manus Islands. It then secured the Admiralty Islands by mid-May 1944, where Chet was wounded in combat.

On 1 June 1944, Ovnand was promoted from first lieutenant to captain on Special Orders No. 131.

It is known that Chester received a Bronze Star for his heroism in the Pacific. Even though the details of the action at the time were classified restricted and few of his military records have survived, one official document shows his signature as Chester M. Ovnand. *

Safeguarding Austria

In 1943, the Allied powers had agreed that Austria would be treated as a liberated country, not as a conquered one. However in 1945, after Austria's liberation, and the end of the war in Europe, the Soviet Union did not honor the agreement. U.S. Army units involved in the liberation of Austria expected to return to the United States when the war ended, although that would not be the case until an individual soldier replacement system was instituted. In October 1947, Captain Ovnand shipped out for Austria from Camp Kilmer, New Jersey. His second wife, Mildred, would later follow.

* Some Internet sites claim that Chester Ovnand was sometimes known as "Charles." There is no evidence, from family or friends, indicating this. All knew him as either Chester or "Chet".

Being of Norwegian descent, growing up in Minnesota, and having done cross country skiing, Chet Ovnand was immediately recognized as a natural for the 3d Army Mountain Ski School at Garmisch-Partenkrirchen, Germany. He was expedited to one of the last classes conducted by the Third Army in the mountains of Bavaria. The Third Army was scheduled to return stateside in 1947 and the school was soon to be reorganized and redesignated. It was considered an important school because, if the Russians had tried to take Western Europe, those skilled in mountain skiing would act as a stop gap force in the mountainous regions between the east and west. Chet was attending the ski school when he and his wife, Mildred, were reunited in late November 1947.

General Mark Clark, the first appointee to the position of U.S. High Commissioner and Commander of U.S. Forces Austria departed, and Lieutenant General Geoffrey Keyes replaced him. Austria was divided into four zones of occupation: U.S., British, French, and Russian. Captain Ovnand wore the red and white "Austria" shoulder patch bearing both sword and olive branch, symbolizing 'peace but prepared for war' which was authorized for wear on 18 August 1945. At first, Chet and Mildred were at Camp McCauley, near Linz in Upper Austria at the Danube River, which served as the border between American and Russian Troops. At the NCO Academy of the U.S. Forces Austria Tactical Command, "He was the personnel officer and an instructor," said Mildred. Later, during his tour, Captain Ovnand was needed at a new location and the couple moved south to Zell-am-See, in the Salzburg Region. The Ovnands never saw Austria without the Russians at their backs. They left in 1951. It was not until 1955 that the Soviet Union signed a treaty ending Russian occupation of Austria. Consequently, U.S. Forces Austria left shortly thereafter, although some U.S. units wore the U.S. Forces Austria patch in Europe until 27 June 1958.

Reduction in Force (RIF)

When the Ovnands left Austria, Captain Ovnand was given a choice: Leave the service as an armor officer who had served his country honorably and faithfully during World War II, or remain in the military as an enlisted man. Chet said to Millie, "Mrs. O., do you mind if I reenlist? I may go back in as a buck-private!"

The military cutback was known as the RIF and Captain Ovnand, choosing to stay in the Army, was reduced in rank to master sergeant (E-7).

Korean Service

In 1951, the Ovnand couple spent a year at Fort Sheridan, Illinois. "He went to Fort Sheridan as First Sergeant, Headquarters Company, U.S. Army Garrison," said Mildred. Initially, Chester Ovnand worked for the post commander, Colonel John Naser, and later in July 1951 for Colonel Stephen E. Bullock. "When the Korean War broke out, he told me, 'You better start packing. I'll be gone in thirty days.'" She told him, "If you go to war, I'm going back to work."

Master Sergeant Chester Ovnand while first sergeant of U.S. Garrison, Fort Sheridan, Illinois
Courtesy of John Sheridan

Rather than being assigned to Korea, Chet Ovnand was sent to Panama, while Mildred went to work at the West Fort Hood, Texas Service Club, then known as Killeen Army Base. Chet wrote to

Millie saying, "Panama is no place for a single man." He requested a transfer and briefly returned stateside, long enough to visit his daughter, Margaret Ann, twelve years old at the time. Reportedly, it was the last time he ever saw her. Immediately after a short leave, he was assigned to Korea. "He spent nine months on the front lines and then came back to Fort Hood for nine months," said Mildred.

It appears that on 28 October 1952, Chester Ovnand was appointed, under Section 37 of the National Defense Act, as a Major in the Armed Forces Reserve. Recognizing him as a warrior, the U.S. Army needed him in combat situations, however, just as soon as the Korean War was over, he again reverted to master sergeant.

One day Chet came home and said, "Mrs. O., there are only two places I haven't been: the China area and Alaska." He left for Southeast Asia on 31 October 1958, telling his wife that he was going to Indochina to help train soldiers in tank warfare.

Indochina Becomes Viet-Nam

"Ovnand was one of the first advisors to be assigned to our new location at Bien Hoa," said Howard Boston.

"He was the first sergeant at MAAG 7 and arrived in, either, October or November of 1958. We were on eleven-month tours back then, but, of course, they told us we'd be in Vietnam for a full year. Officially we were not assigned as U.S. military advisors at regimental level until May 1959 but, I believe, Chet went up to Bien Hoa from Saigon a couple of weeks early. Before that, all the advisors were assigned to Saigon, although we'd regularly visit the ARVN units at their bases on inspection tours."

"Chet was a knowledgeable man and a good soldier. When something was wrong he was the kind of guy who wanted to fix it," said Howard Boston. "He was generally soft-spoken, but on one inspection visit to Duc My, Chet strongly advised the officer-in-charge of the team, to report some real problems the Vietnamese unit was having. In the final version of the written report, there was no mention of the troubles and/or failures of the ARVN unit. The popular consensus among the officers was, 'If you don't have a good report for General Sam Williams, you'd better keep your mouth shut and not say anything at all.' Chet really disagreed with that policy, but his boss wouldn't budge on the flowery report.

"I mentioned Chet was generally soft spoken, but he sure stood his ground on the accuracy in reporting issue. I guess, his stand on the matter might have been one of the reasons he ended up in Bien Hoa early.

"The policy of 'no bad report cards' came to a head later in 1959 when LTC Bergen B. Hovell, an advisor to I Corps, felt compelled to speak out about the problem, but, I really believe, Chet was the guy who initially took issue with keeping negative reports from General 'Hanging Sam' Williams."

"On Wednesday afternoon, 8 July 1959, exactly two months to the day after my arrival at the BIF Compound," said Victor Gorlinsky, "Master Sergeant Ovnand and I were sitting on one of the screen enclosed porches discussing our World War II experiences – normally we played horse shoes on Wednesday afternoons, but there were no horseshoes played on that day. It was raining heavily. Sergeant Ovnand was an infantry soldier in the South Pacific during World War II. He knew combat. I had little to offer for discussion, other than my service thirty miles behind the lines in Belgium during the Battle of the Bulge. I admired Sergeant Ovnand very much, and others in the detachment did also. He and Captain Boston were good friends."

In July 2012, Vic Gorlinsky told me, "As well as I knew Chet Ovnand, he never once mentioned to me that he held reserve officer status, fought as an officer in combat, was awarded a Bronze Star and Purple Heart, or had been rifted back down to the enlisted ranks after serving in two wars. He wasn't about airs and graces, but about doing his job to the best of his ability. He'd prove that, in spades, later that night. After our conversation we had dinner, then we set up the movie projector in the dining room. It's the last time I would see Chet alive."

Chapter 8
The BIF Compound

MAAG 7's main building, looking from the front of the BIF Compound. To the left is the cook's family quarters, and to the right, the kitchen and covered causeway.
Photographs courtesy of LTC Victor W. Gorlinsky, US Army (ret.)

The BIF Compound was occupied by MAAG personnel throughout American involvement in Vietnam from 1959 through 1973. It got its unusual name because standing at the main building's entrance, looking down to one's right, there was a big water tower painted with the letters B I F, which stood for *Bureau Industrielle Forestier* - the French Forestry Service. Lumber had been an important commodity to the French in Indochina.

In a short story which I encountered, published in 1981, it was explained that the attack occurred "...inside a gray stucco saw-mill recently converted to an American mess hall..." However, the actual sawmill barns were a few hundred feet in either direction from the BIF main building where the attack occurred.

Fortunately, Victor Gorlinsky took photographs of most of the buildings located on the MAAG 7 compound in 1959.

"Our large, two story main building, the former French planters residence, was a combination mess hall and day room, and had a bar and a store room at one end. It had a double roof configuration, and shutters and screens on all the windows," said Vic. "It was about one-hundred yards from the Dong Nai River, and before the attack there were no defenses between us and the river bank."

The back of the main building as seen from the Viet Cong's river approach. The kitchen is to the left and the cook's family quarters to the right. A VC sniper positioned himself at the second window from the right. LTC Victor W. Gorlinsky, US Army (ret.)

"The photos of the BIF Compound, taken in 1959, show the front and back of the main building which served as the dining room on the ground floor and several rooms on the second floor used as quarters. M/Sgt Ovnand's quarters and visiting guest quarters were on the second floor. To the right of the building in the front photograph was the kitchen and power room. We had two generators there. The building to the left was where our first cook, Mr. Bai, and his family lived. To the rear of the main building was mostly open space that went back to the Dong Nai River."

Looking from the front porch of the main building, to the right is the road leading out of the BIF Compound beyond a small Sago palm. To the left, behind the large Banyan tree, are the quarters of Captains Beau Turner and Victor Gorlinsky.

The third picture [above], taken from the front of the main building, shows the quarters behind the Banyan tree, where Beau Turner and Gorlinsky lived. To the left, buildings for the security platoon and a garage for the colonel's sedan. The colonel's quarters are behind these buildings. From the main building, Captain Boston's and Major Hallett's quarters were located to the right of the driveway."

Based on calculations from Victor Gorlinsky's photographs and recollections, the main building was approximately thirty-five feet long by twenty-two feet wide. On the ground floor, complemented by slow turning ceiling fans, was a bar area, a storeroom, a projector and table, four sofas, a large dining table and chairs, a movie screen, and a shelf near the side door. The main building had two doorways, one set of double doors opening outward at the front of the building, and a single side doorway. In addition to shutters, the side door had a swinging screen door which opened either way, as did the door to the actual kitchen itself. Both doors were under the covered causeway connecting the two buildings. This was where a Viet Cong sapper positioned himself during the attack.

The BIF water tower as seen from the 7th ARVN Division's compound. From this angle, the letters B I F cannot be seen. LTC Victor W. Gorlinsky, US Army (ret.)

"Bien Hoa Industrielle et Forestiere Maison de Planteur"
The BIF area at Bien Hoa during the time of French occupation French Archives

Chapter 9
The Blind Men and the Elephant

MAAG 7 officers from left to right - LTC Ellsworth Davis, and carrying .45's Major James "Jack" Hallett, Captain Edward Beauregard Turner and Captain Victor Gorlinsky, after weapons were authorized subsequent to the 1959 attack. Photo courtesy of LTC Victor W. Gorlinsky, US Army (ret.)

In addition to Captain Howard Boston, Captain Victor Gorlinsky, Major Dale Buis and Master Sergeant Chester Ovnand, two other individuals were present in the main building during the attack—Colonel Clay and Major Jack D. Hallett. Others were interviewed or mentioned in press reports as having knowledge of what had happened. They were either members of MAAG Headquarters, MAAG 5, or MAAG 7.

A brief description of all individuals present during the attack, or those later interviewed, follows:

Captain Howard B. Boston, Artillery advisor, MAAG 7, was present during the attack. He was seated on the back couch, closest to the front window, to the right of Captain Victor Gorlinsky. Boston was the first American shot on the night of the attack.

Captain Victor W. Gorlinsky, Signal Corps advisor, MAAG 7, was present during the attack. Captain Gorlinsky was seated to the left of Howard Boston and the closest man to Sergeant Ovnand and the movie projector.

Master Sergeant Chester M. Ovnand, 1st Sergeant, MAAG 7, was present during the attack. He was operating the movie projector. M/Sgt Ovnand was the second American shot that night.

Major Dale R. Buis, Infantry, visiting MAAG 7 from MAAG 5, was present during the attack. Major Buis sat at a large wooden dining table to the left of the projector and Sergeant Ovnand. He was in a direct line to the side door, 20 feet away, leading to the kitchen house. Major Buis was the third American shot that night.

Colonel Clay, Senior Advisor MAAG 5, a visitor to MAAG 7, was present during the attack. Victor Gorlinsky remarked, "I'd describe Colonel Clay, the senior advisor at MAAG 5 with us that night, as being in his 50's, thin, about six feet with a full head of dark hair and a regulation military hair cut. He was only at Bien Hoa briefly. MAAG seemed to make an effort to eliminate him from any reports or anything to do with the attack once it was over. More than one report stated that there were only five of us in the building when we were hit, although we were actually six including Colonel Clay."

Major James "Jack" Hallett, Infantry, MAAG 7, was present during the attack. "Jack Hallett was seated to Colonel Clay's left when the firing started," said Victor Gorlinsky. "Most everything written about him in the press involving that night should be taken with a grain of salt." Hallett's name was used in several stories about the attack, yet most of the things he was said to have done were conjecture or fabrication.

Captain Edward Beauregard Turner, Engineer Officer, MAAG 7, was absent during the attack. "Beau Turner, from South Carolina, was military to the core. Tennis was a passion with him. He'd often skip dinner so he could get to the courts early, usually pairing up with, or playing against French civilians. With his regular tennis schedule going on, naturally, he wasn't at the movie that night, but later returned to assist."

Standing in front of Boston's and Hallett's quarters (left to right) are LTC Ellsworth Davis, an unidentified advisor, Captain Howard Boston, Major E. Beau Turner and M/Sgt Ovnand's replacement 1SG Bourdon. LTC Victor Gorlinsky, US Army (ret.)

LTC Ellsworth Davis, Infantry, Acting Senior Advisor MAAG 7, was absent during the attack. LTC Davis, an easy going, decent officer was filling the slot as Senior Advisor to MAAG 7, but was, in fact, the Deputy Senior Advisor until his replacement arrived. LTC Davis was in his room during the attack.

Major Charles Watson, Infantry Advisor, MAAG 7, was absent during the attack. Vic Gorlinsky remembered, "Charles Watson was a first-rate infantry officer who served in Europe during World War II. After dinner he'd often grab a six-pack of beer and head to his room. He had married a British girl, and spent a lot of his off-duty time in his quarters writing home to his wife and his family."

Colonel Huynh Van Cao, Commander of the 7th ARVN Division, was not present during the attack. Cao's headquarters was a short distance from the advisory compound. Colonel Cao was on a first name basis with the American advisors at MAAG 7, who supported his military efforts in the III Corps area.

Colonel Charles A. Symroski, MAAG Intelligence Officer, was not present during the attack. Colonel Symroski interviewed Victor Gorlinsky and Beau Turner after the attack. Based on his interviews, a report was written and shortly thereafter released to the news media, making it appear as though Gorlinsky had been interviewed by news reporters, when he had not been.

Col Nathaniel P. Ward III, US Army
Photo courtesy of Captain Nathaniel P. Ward IV, USA (ret.)

Colonel Nathaniel P. Ward III, Chief of the Vietnamese Command, was not present during the attack, but was the first officer from MAAG Headquarters to arrive on the scene at Bien Hoa later that evening. In 1991 he made several detailed comments about his observations, which Victor Gorlinsky later put into context.

Like the "blind men and the elephant" described in John Godfrey Saxe's poem, each of the mentioned individuals would have had their own account of the attack, but only Boston's, Gorlinsky's, and Ward's would come to light.

Chapter 10
Reel Change

Several days before the attack, Captain Victor Gorlinsky awaits the start of a movie. This is the only known photograph of the interior of the BIF main building. Photo taken by M/Sgt Chester M. Ovnand courtesy LTC Victor W. Gorlinsky, US Army (ret.)

The 8th of July 1959 was a moonless night. It had rained hard late that afternoon and although the rain had stopped, there was still heavy cloud cover. A small band of determined Viet Cong, armed with a variety of rudimentary weapons, quietly approached the Bien Hoa MAAG Compound in two boats from Dong Nai Island.

This Viet Cong attack had been planned at a quarterly meeting of communist leaders in April 1959. Their plan was simple and at the time of its conception was thought to be effective. Waiting in their boats, just a few hundred yards offshore from the compound, when the VC would see the lights doused in the main building they would quietly paddle to the river bank and kill American advisors relaxing inside. As in all Viet Cong terrorist operations, only one or two

Six Vietnamese children approach the BIF Compound, along the shore of the Dong Nai River. The three flat ladder steps in the foreground were those by which the Viet Cong gained entrance to the area. Photos by LTC Victor W.Gorlinsky, US Army (ret.)

A boat like those used to transport the Viet Cong, prior to the attack. "Small boats like this were everywhere on the Dong Nai River," said Vic Gorlinsky.

men at the top knew all the planned details.

"We always ate early on Wednesdays," said Victor Gorlinsky. "After our evening meal when it was still daylight, Beau Turner, who was dressed to play tennis, went off to the Bien Hoa tennis courts. Most everyone else was wearing slacks, button up sport shirts, loafers, or sandals, which was the 'uniform' after 4:30 P.M. Shortly after supper, LTC Ellsworth Davis and Major Charles Watson retired to their rooms."

One of the opening frames from the Universal International movie *The Tattered Dress*
Hollywood Movie Stills - Tom Conroy

Inside the main building, Captain Victor Gorlinsky turned out the lights and took his seat next to Captain Howard Boston, as Chet Ovnand hit the switch on the movie projector. The black and white 1957 movie opened with the Universal International turning globe, then a wrap-around style trademark proclaiming "Cinemascope," which the MAAG projector was equipped with an additional special lens to accommodate. Cameo flashes of Jeff Chandler, Jeanne Crain, Jack Carson, and Gail Russell appeared on the screen. Charleen Reston, played by Elaine Stewart, stood in front of a table lamp in an otherwise darkened room. There was an ash tray with a smoldering cigarette and a bottle of whiskey. She took a drink from her glass and as she did, she had the rear portion of her evening gown torn down her back from the hand of an unseen man lying on a bed. She turned her head and at first, surprised, she smiled as the title of the movie, *The Tattered Dress,* appeared across the screen.

The movie lights flickered through the windows, as the Viet Cong approached the shore, while the movie continued with a close-up of a smirking Charleen Reston driving her sports car as a desert road backdrop disappeared behind her.

Within those first minutes of the movie flickering in the main building, the Viet Cong docked their boats in the mud. They saw no one at the back of the main building and realized that any military guards would have been at the windows at the front.

Based on traces of muddy footprints found later, the raiding party scurried across an open area and circled wide. The Viet Cong surrounded the main building on both sides. One team encompassed the kitchen building, and came up behind a guard, a mess assistant, and a young boy, all of whom had been outside peering through the right front windows to catch a glimpse of the movie.

More VC took up their positions, as they poked weapons through their assigned windows, under the cover of Jeff Chandler's deep voice and Frank Skinner's musical score.

The first raider positioned himself at the back of the main building with his weapon aimed through the second window from the right, close to where Major Dale Buis was seated at a dining table. A second raider positioned a STEN machinegun through a window at the end of the building.

The Viet Cong cell leader took up a position at the front of the main building, through the second window from the left, to the right side of the sofa on which Captain Boston and Captain Gorlinsky were seated, aiming his weapon at Captain Boston's face.

Chester Ovnand had his back to the window closest to the cook's quarters - the window where the STEN machinegun was placed.

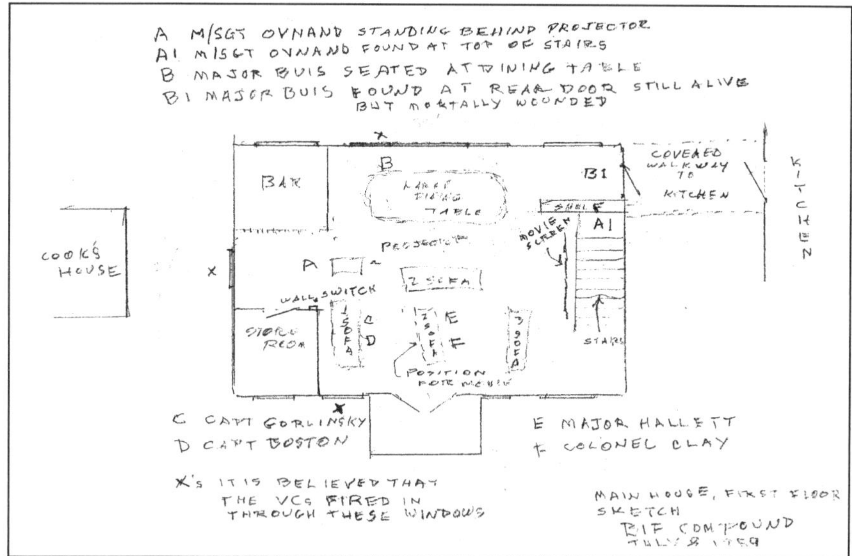

Victor Gorlinsky's original sketch of the main building where six advisors were located at the time the Viet Cong opened fire. Viet Cong are indicated by X's outside the building. Courtesy of LTC Victor W. Gorlinsky, US Army (ret.)

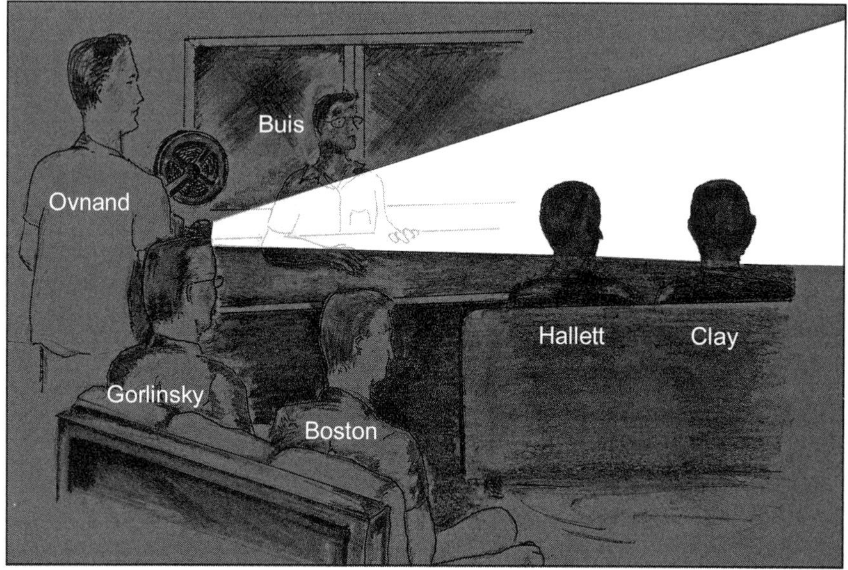

Based on Victor Gorlinsky's detailed description, this depiction shows who was where in the main building prior to the opening Viet Cong salvo.

"The last thing I remember about the movie was Jack Carson riding in a jeep talking to Jeff Chandler about football saying, 'I'll never forget one night in my sleep - I busted out of bed like I was going for a long pass and crashed into a window,'" said Howard Boston. "It was twenty minutes into the film when the reel clattered to an end. When Sergeant Ovnand turned on the lights, I saw the first flash come from outside the window immediately to my right. I got hit by that first round fired - it hit me below the nostril. I went down instantly and got as close to the floor as I could."

After the Viet Cong cell leader discharged his first round, gun fire erupted in the building from three windows on the south side. Over the din, someone shouted, "Everyone hit the deck!"

"I was loosing blood but I never lost consciousness," said Boston. "The firing seemed to come from everywhere. It was coming cross-fire, from both sides and from behind us."

Even in two separate bursts it took only moments for the first 32 round clip of ammunition to be expended from the STEN. What the STEN machine-gunner behind Chester Ovnand had not counted on, was that he did not have a 180 degree radius of fire. Although Ovnand's back was directly in front of him, the bar was to the gunner's left and the storeroom to his right which obstructed the view of the entire room. Even though the Viet Cong had received some intelligence, because entry to the main building was restricted to only a handful of Vietnamese, there had been no report about the layout of the interior. This oversight severely limited the STEN's effectiveness, further complicated by the fact that it was in the hands of an operator incapable of keeping it aimed down to fire at targets waist high or lower. Everything happened in seconds.

STEN 9mm rounds rose up, higher and higher, into the far wall where the stair case, the movie screen, and the side door were. For a few short moments, rounds chopped at the inside of the building, but most of the firing was ineffective.

Master Sergeant Ovnand was hit first in the abdomen, then in the neck by the STEN volley coming from the back window, while

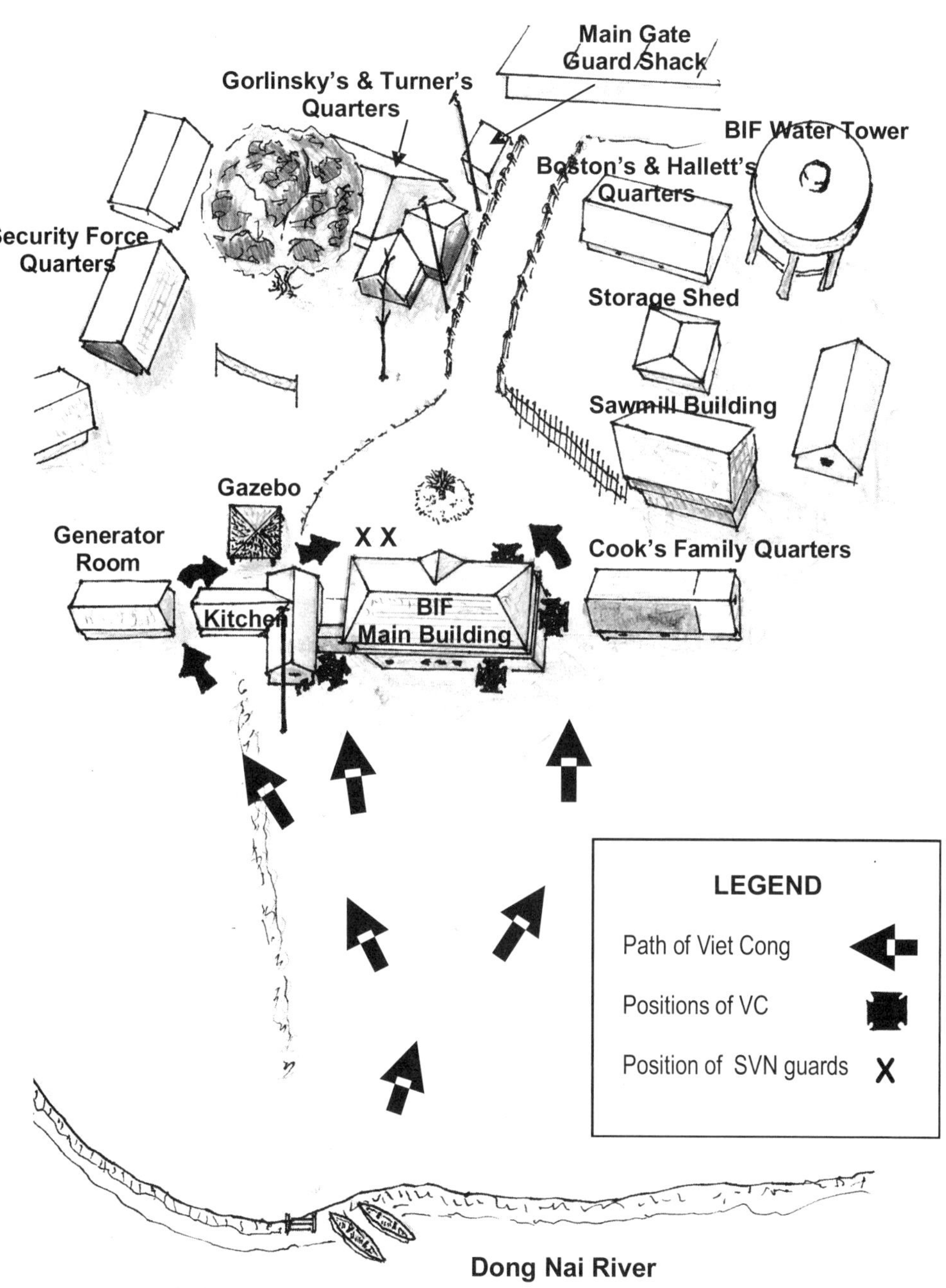

The BIF Compound on the night of the 8 July 1959 attack

one 9mm round ricocheted off the movie projector. Ignoring his wounds, Ovnand managed to turn out the interior lights, giving cover to the four advisors who had been sitting to the right of the movie projector and who were now on the floor. His actions made Colonel Clay, Major Hallett, Captain Gorlinsky, and Captain Boston no easy targets. The darkened room also concealed Major Buis, crouched between the back wall and the large dining table.

As soon as the cell leader had fired his pistol at Boston, he turned his attention to the outside of the building, firing multiple rounds to his right as part of the cross fire which killed one guard, one mess attendant and put three rounds in the chest of the mess cook's son.

When Boston was hit by the first well aimed "signal round" and dropped to the floor, the unscathed Captain Gorlinsky slid off the couch, not moving a muscle, lying on his back hoping that in the darkness he would not be detected by any of the attackers. "For a moment, I laid there frozen," said Vic.

Dale Buis had been sitting at the dining table when the firing started and he instinctively hit the floor. Although severely bleeding Chet Ovnand, after turning out the lights, bolted passed the couch where Boston and Gorlinsky had been seated, then passed the couch where Hallett and Clay had been. He covered twenty-five feet across the room and mounted the stairs to the second floor.

Chet recognized that the only chance to break the attack, coming from the outside of the building, was to hit the exterior flood lights which would illuminate the compound. He was the only one who knew where the upstairs light switch was, because it was his job to turn them on every night.

"Somewhere at the top of the stairs was a switch for the outside lights. Chet wanted to get those lights on. I couldn't have told you where the switch was," said Gorlinsky. "I was the mess officer, but I had never been on the second floor of the main building at any time during my two months in Vietnam. Normally, Chet didn't turn those lights on until later in the evening when things had settled down and people were going to bed. He made it to the second floor, amongst the deafening firing and the smell of cordite, and only after he had succeeded in turning on the outside lights did he collapse at the top of the stairs. Turning on the flood lights was a major factor in breaking the attack. At the time, we didn't know what he was up to, or where he was."

Chet Ovnand while stationed in Austria
Photo courtesy of John Sheridan

Dale Buis while stationed in Japan
Courtesy of the Buis family

Major Buis, encompassed in darkness inside the main building on the ground floor, crawled towards the kitchen door. He saw a shadowy figure outside in the causeway illuminated when the flood lights came on. Recognizing the shadow as another attacker, he darted fifteen feet, and while under fire, made it to the doorway.

In a split second, Buis could see the VC preparing a satchel charge which he was about to throw through the doorway into the main building, and he confronted the sapper. The VC defensively backed-up just as a round from the uncontrollable and rising STEN machine gun came from the far back window and caught Dale Buis in the back of the head.

Major Buis had confounded the sapper long enough for the sapper to hesitate. In the split-second confusion the sapper, who had already activated the satchel charge, did not have time to throw it before it detonated with a deafening blast. The explosion cut the sapper's body in two. The upper half of the enemy's body was shredded into pieces and thrown 100 feet in a 180 degree arc. The explosion also threw Colonel Clay's sedan back six feet and totaled it.

"I had wanted to crawl for the big round, heavy oak dining table," said Boston, "but I realized that I couldn't make it on my own."

The Vietnamese first assistant cook stands at the kitchen under the covered causeway, only a few feet from where the sapper stood when the satchel charge exploded. The jeep is parked where Colonel Clay's sedan was when it was totaled. LTC Victor Gorlinsky, USA (ret.)

"From what I could see among the flashes," said Boston, "Buis made his way across the room, pushed open the door leading to the kitchen building, and startled one of the terrorists getting ready to throw a bomb into the main room. The bomb went off in the doorway killing the raider which saved the rest of us. If it hadn't been for Buis and Ovnand, none of us would have survived that night."

"As soon as the firing stopped," Boston said, "Vic who was lying on his back, rolled over and dragged me in the direction of cover."

"There was a small supply room opposite the bar, a little bigger than a closet," said Vic. "This was where I dragged Blackie once the firing stopped. I was able to move him into the supply room, which had limited the STEN's arc of fire, and tried to make him comfortable. I propped his head up and lessened the bleeding with some towels."

"If it weren't for Vic, I probably would have bled to death," said Boston. "He elevated my head on a case of beer and staunched the bleeding coming from my face."

After he had attended to Boston, Gorlinsky went looking for other wounded. "Major Buis had been hit by a round, he must have backed up a step or two, and dropped over backwards into the doorway where I found him," said Vic. "When I got to him, his eyes were closed and his head was lying in a pool of blood." Gorlinsky continued, "He was quite bloodied and it was hard to tell where all the blood was coming from, but I could see he had been hit from behind. His face was illuminated by the outside flood lights which helped me find the pulse in his carotid artery which was throbbing. At first it didn't occur to me where Sergeant Ovnand was, or what he had done, but with two men severely bleeding on the ground floor, I knew I had to get medical help immediately."

"There was no evidence that the South Vietnamese guards ever fired any shots – it was pitch black – they couldn't have seen enemy targets coming from behind them. The VC were gone as soon as the outside flood lights came on and the explosion occurred," said Vic Gorlinsky.

When the satchel charge exploded it became apparent to the attackers that their well thought-out plans had gone miserably array and they fled after the satchel detonation. The STEN gun proved ineffective in the wrong hands - they had not killed all the Americans. One of their men had been unsuccessful in getting his satchel charge into the building. Worse still, he had blown himself up in the process while possibly wounding a second attacker.

"Things were confused and I suffered ear damage," said Boston.

"Lying in the store room, I heard muffled chatter and I thought it was 'Colonel Clay' trying to get through to his unit on the phone. He sounded agitated."

"It wasn't the colonel," said Vic. "It was me. After I checked Major Buis, I got on the field phone and tried to rouse 7th ARVN Headquarters next door. I began shouting 'Help!' 'Help!' 'Help!' figuring, whomever the Vietnamese on the other end of the line was, those words might be something they'd understand."

Colonel Huynh Van Cao stands in front of the road from which he led a 7th ARVN Division relief force, consisting of soldiers and an ambulance, minutes after the July attack. LTC Victor W. Gorlinsky, US Army (ret.)

"When I wasn't absolutely sure I had made myself understood that we needed immediate assistance from the ARVNs, I went out the front door and jumped in a jeep. My plan was to get to the ARVN compound as fast as I could and bring back help. What I didn't realize was that the Vietnamese guards, who lived in our compound had heard the firing and had already gotten word to them. Not knowing that, I drove down the road towards their compound with my lights off, but didn't get more than 100 yards when I saw Colonel Huynh Van Cao and a group of his soldiers, and medics coming through our gate. I threw the jeep in reverse and went back to the main building to see where I could help."

Although it only took a few minutes for Vietnamese medical personnel to get there to attend to Major Buis, he had already succumbed to his wounds. "They found Chet at the top of the stairs," said Vic. "Both men had bled to death."

The Vietnamese took Blackie from the storeroom to the ambulance and the medics bandaged him up so tightly that he had nothing more than a small hole in the bandages, through which he had just enough room to breath.

"By this time, Beau Turner had made his way back from his tennis match. We grabbed his shotgun and while the medics were working on Boston and the young boy, Beau and I inspected all the buildings for enemy presence," Vic said. "After Blackie was bandaged, the two of us put him in the back of LTC Davis' sedan. Beau drove while I sat in the back seat holding Boston's head on my chest.

"Once we arrived at the dispensary in Saigon, we stayed until we were told that Boston was out of danger. Then Beau and I went to the Brink BOQ to spend the night. When we got to the Brink, Colonel Charles Symroski* MAAG's intelligence officer, was waiting for us. He had questions about the attack and what had happened. We spent a bit of time with him, then got quarters for the night, and drove back to Bien Hoa the next morning."

At least forty-two enemy rounds were fired during the attack, one (1) round hit Major Howard Boston; two (2) 9mm rounds hit Master Sergeant Ovnand, one in the abdomen, and then as the STEN rose up, a second hit Ovnand in the neck; while another one (1) struck the movie projector; three (3) rounds hit the mess cook's son; one (1) STEN round hit Major Buis; and thirty-two (32) STEN machinegun rounds lodged in the far wall through the movie screen.

* Colonel Charles Albert Symroski, joined Headquarters MAAG Vietnam in 1958, and held the position as senior intelligence officer G-2 until 1960.

There was no evidence that any rounds hit the floor as reported in one news account. At least two (2) rounds, one round each, hit the two Vietnamese soldiers who were outside.

It was reported that the two Vietnamese soldiers, in an "ensuing gun battle" were shot and killed. Victor Gorlinsky is certain that the ARVNs did not return fire during the raid.

One report stated, "As soon as he hit the deck, Buis crawled across the room and forced open the door, his fellow officers said. This startled one of the terrorists, who was getting ready to throw a bomb… The bomb went off in the doorway, killing both Buis and the raider."

"Although Beau and I were mentioned by name in that story and I was quoted as saying, 'It cost Buis his life but it saved the others,'" said Vic Gorlinsky, "I recall no such interview. It was because I had been the one who had given the MAAG intelligence officer, Colonel Symroski, a first hand account that my name seemed to be out there for the press to use as they saw fit. Three things are for certain: (1) only Howard Boston saw Major Buis make it to the doorway; (2) Buis was in a full standing position at the doorway when he was hit; and (3) he was hit by a STEN round coming through the back window, not by the explosion."

The only Viet Cong killed that night was the one confronted by Major Buis.

The scene at the mess hall was reported as, "a wreck, with blood-stains on the floor. The bullet-shattered film projector, with one large bent metal reel, swung crazily. A letter written [by Sergeant Ovnand] to his wife was still in the mess room mailbox."

The only problem with the report was that Buis was not killed by the explosion, and the mail box had been invented by the press.

Chapter 11
Major Jack D. Hallett

Major Jack D. Hallett, US Army
LTC Victor W. Gorlinsky, US Army (ret.)

Major Jack D. Hallett had been assigned to MAAG 7 as one of its senior infantry advisors since November 1958. He was a rough and rugged officer from Baton Rouge, Louisiana, who had been a member of the 104th Infantry Division during World War II. In the autumn of 1944, his division fought across Germany from the Battle of Hurtgen Forest, the longest battle of the war on German soil, until 26 April 1945, when at Pretzsch - Wittemberg, Germany, the 104th linked up with the Soviet Army. As a young officer, Hallett had been one of the first eyewitnesses to the inhumanity of the Nazis at the death camp at Nordhausen, where he saw the results of the extermination of ill prisoners who died of starvation and total lack of medical care.

In early 1945, soldiers of the 104th Infantry Division (Timber Wolves) move through a German city shortly before the close of the war. US Army photo courtesy I. Johnson

On the night of the attack on Bien Hoa, Hallett was sitting with Colonel Clay, MAAG 5 chief, to the right of the movie screen when the firing erupted. One news report indicated that it was Major Hallett who shouted "Hit the deck!" Then during a lull in the firing, he "dashed out the front door" and reportedly "slugged a couple of the communists on the way out..." His actions on the night of 8 July 1959 are vague, but not totally unknown. Major Hallett died in 1997 before he could be interviewed for this book.

The news account in which he was attributed as (1) shouting "Hit the deck!" is possible; (2) accrediting him as jumping over Chet Ovnand to turn out lights is not likely. Hallett was sitting close to the movie screen and was no where near the light switch next to the movie projector; (3) Reporters had Hallett dashing out the main door and driving off to Saigon for help which made no sense and which he did not do. It was Vic Gorlinsky who jumped in a jeep and drove towards the 7th ARVN Compound to get medical help; (4) Hallett was also reported to have slugged a couple of Viet Cong as he left the scene of the attack, which someone had to have assumed based on the original message to General Williams which stated, "One advisor had physical contact outside building with one attacker." According to Howard Boston that "one advisor" was Major Buis who had prevented the sapper from launching his satchel charge. No one went out the front door of the building until after the attack had stopped and the Viet Cong had gone.

After the attack, Major Jack Hallett wears a .45 caliber pistol over his shoulder as he stands with two security guards near the back door of the main building. Through the causeway a 4 foot high fence, installed after the attack, is visible. LTC Gorlinsky, USA (ret.)

There are no complete details as to what actions Major Hallett took immediately after the attack. In the confusion and darkness his exact whereabouts were not known, but according to Vic Gorlinsky, in Vic's brief absence, upon the arrival of Colonel Cao's medical personnel, Major Hallett, who had first realized that Sergeant Ovnand had died at the top of the stairs, directed the Vietnamese medics to the locations of those that had been hit - Boston in the store room - Buis at the side door - Ovnand at the top of the stairs.

Victor Gorlinsky characterized Jack Hallett as a calm, easy going and honest officer who had strong feelings about what was right and wrong. After stories about the attack were published in the media, Major Hallett could see that some stories describing his involvement had been written out of context and had alleged he had performed actions during the attack which he had not. After one weekly magazine published such a story, Major Hallett attempted to set the record straight but was stone-walled. By the time he had seen the story it was already old news, a mute point, and no news people were interested in his corrections. The weekly magazine chose not to print any revisions and the story stood.

Major Jack D. Hallett waterskiing on the Dong Nai River
Photo courtesy of LTC Victor Gorlinsky, US Army (ret.)

Major Hallett left Vietnam in November 1959 and was not in country when others were asked to testify about the attack. Jack D. Hallett was born on 11 August 1918. After his retirement from the U.S. Army he lived in Myrtle Beach, South Carolina, where he died on 6 December 1997. He is buried at Arlington National Cemetery, Virginia.

Chapter 12
Message Traffic After the Attack

Many officials visited MAAG 7 after the July attack. Congressman, Daniel J. Flood (D) Pennsylvania, stands at the main building gesturing skyward as his military escort from MAAG Saigon looks on. LTC Victor W. Gorlinsky, USA (ret.)

The large dining table was the only raised area that could support the weight of two bodies. Major Buis and Master Sergeant Ovnand were wrapped appropriately, and placed on the table as MAAG 7 awaited mortuary personnel to take them to Saigon in the morning.

"When Beau Turner and I got back to Bien Hoa, I was told that LTC Davis, Major Hallett and Major Watson took shifts sitting up all night with the bodies. Vietnamese maintenance people were already patching up bullet holes in the walls," said Vic. "I don't know if the raiders had broken through the screens covering the windows, or had lifted them, because the maintenance crew from Saigon was already putting heavy screen mesh on all the downstairs windows, so there would not be a repeat of the incident, and so grenades couldn't be thrown through any windows. A single four-foot-high fence was being strung between the river and the billeting area, thirty feet behind the main building."

The repairs and security upgrades had been prompted by a message dispatched by Headquarters MAAG to all advisory detachments at 03:25 A.M. on 9 July:

> CONFIDENTIAL
>
> 2025Z 8 July 1959
>
> CHMAAG Vietnam
>
> Senior Advisors
> All Advisor Detachments
>
> 66∅
>
> Confidential MAGAG.PO ____________
>
> 1. 7th Div Adv Det Mess at Bien Hoa attacked at 1900 hours 8 July. Assailants used automatic weapons and improvised bomb. Attack made during showing of movie when lights were on during changing reels. Two advisors killed and one wounded.
>
> 2. Verify adequacy of security measures for your Detachment. . .
>
> ROBERT H. CUSHING, JR.
> Capt, Armor
> Staff Duty Officer

Colonel Nathaniel P. Ward, Chief of the Vietnamese Command said, "After seeing the results of the attack at MAAG 7 first-hand, I returned to Headquarters MAAG in Saigon. The duty officer, Captain Cushing; LTC Symroski and I, along with a few others, were up most of the night dispatching messages; deciding what action to take in advising outlying MAAG detachments about the attack; and waiting for General Williams to return. Notification of the deaths went to the Pentagon, so that the families could be notified."

In Copperas Cove, Texas, on 9 July, Mildred Ovnand was getting ready for work as she sipped her coffee. Half watching television, she heard on the *Today Show* that two soldiers had been killed at Bien Hoa, Vietnam, but the names of those killed were being withheld pending notification of the families. Moments later the phone rang and a *Dallas Associated Press* reporter asked her, "When did you first hear about your husband's death?"

In Chula Vista, California, when the Buis family was notified of Dale's death, the household erupted in grief and chaos. "I only knew something awful had happened," said the eldest son Kurt. "A doctor came in and gave my mother a sedative." An aunt took Kurt and his two brothers for a ride in the family car. It was a way to get them away from the house, and to break the news to them.

On 9 July 1959, Doctor L. James Buis received a telegram from his brother, Harold, notifying him of their brother's death which read:

> Dale shot by unidentified Assailant and Died July 8th Vietnam - Stop - No Further Details. Harold

Back in Vietnam, soldiers and local police began scouring the immediate countryside and investigating any leads about potential perpetrators of the attack. In the South Vietnamese Army's search for the terrorists, it was reported that several suspects were arrested, Thursday, 9 July, less than 24 hours after the assault on the BIF Compound. However, after being interrogated they were released.

On 10 July 1959, a United Press International (UPI) report appeared in the European edition of *The Stars and Stripes*:

> **"2 U.S. Advisors Killed By Vietnam Communists**
>
> "SAIGON (UPI) – Communist terrorists attacking from the jungle threw a plastic bomb into an American Military Advisory Group's

billet near here. In the ensuing blast and exchange of gun fire two Americans, two Vietnamese, and one of the attackers were killed.

"A third American was injured. The Americans killed were Maj. Dale R. Buis of Imperial Beach, Calif. and M/Sgt Chester M. Ovnand of Copperas Cove, Tex.

"Capt., Howard B. Boston of Blairsburg, Iowa, was wounded.

"In Washington, U.S. officials said they are certain the South Vietnam government is doing everything possible to capture the terrorists.

"The attack, one of several instances of recently stepped-up terrorist activities in South Vietnam, occurred shortly after 7 pm during a movie showing.

"Five to 10 men armed with small weapons and a homemade plastic bomb struck from the nearby jungle against the American billet located at Bien Hoa, 20 miles north of Saigon. They threw the bomb, aiming at a window.

"It bounced back, killing one of the attackers. He has been identified definitely as a Communist.

"The remaining attackers then opened fire with small arms which included some automatic weapons.

"Vietnamese guards returned the fire, forcing the terrorists to flee to a nearby river.

"The South Vietnamese Army moved quickly into the area searching the countryside for suspects and making several arrests.

"It was not immediately clear whether the Americans were victims of the bomb or the gun fire.

"Boston was rushed to Saigon for transfer to a hospital in the Philippines. He was reported in serious condition.

"All American military personnel in Saigon were placed on standby alert after the attack.

"Although there have been frequent reports of increased Communist terrorist activities this was the first attack on an American installation in South Vietnam since October 1957, when two bombs were exploded outside a US military billet in the Saigon area and another small bomb was detonated in front of the Information Service Library.

"Some Americans were wounded outside the billet in the 1957 attack but there were no deaths.

"Protest lodged – In another instance of Red terrorism, the South Vietnamese government disclosed it has logged a strong protest with the International Truce Commission against 'reported raids by Communist armed men' in the demilitarized zone between North and South Vietnam. The Saigon government said armed Communist agents apparently forced 73 persons of 17 families into North Vietnam by gunpoint, and then burned houses to prevent their return. The raids occurred in the villages of Trang and Ta Voong."

At least three points were incorrect. The popular consensus was that (1) the bomb had bounced off a screen which it had not; (2) the attackers fired after the bomb exploded which they did not; and (3) the South Vietnamese guards returned fire which they did not.

At the far end of the BIF Compound was a building where LTC Davis' sedan was kept, and beyond it to the right, one of the sawmill buildings where lumber was at one time cut by the French. Photo courtesy of LTC Victor W. Gorlinsky, US Army (ret.)

CONFIDENTIAL

PRIORITY

1101Z 9 July 1959 [18:01 hours local]

CHIEF MAAG VIETNAM

COMMANDER, 6200TH AIR BASE WING,
CLARK AB, P.I.

ATTENTION: MORTUARY OFFICER

665

UNCLAS MAGJS-SB ________

Reference is made to shipment of deceased personnel on MATS Flight #522, 9 July 1959.

Advice is furnished that complete Class "A" uniforms for Major Dale R. Buis.., US Army and M/Sgt Chester M. Ovnand.., reserve Major US Army, are not available for shipment to your organization.

MEMO FOR RECORD:

Uniforms obtained from deceased personnel's quarters at Bien Hoa were not suitable for mortuary purposes therefore they are not being forwarded to Clark AB to accompany remains to CONUS. Uniforms obtained are being turned over to summary court officer.

Walter O. Wylie, Capt.QMC

WILLIAM C. DORN,
Lt Col, AGC
Adjutant General

There was no military mortuary in Vietnam. After the bodies of Master Sergeant Ovnand and Major Buis were sent to the mortuary at Clark Air Base, MAAG Vietnam was still trying to reconstruct what had happened and investigators were at a loss. At 0209Z, 10 July 1959, (0909 A.M. local), the following "Confidential" message was dispatched:

PRIORITY

0209Z 10 JULY 1959

CHMAAG VIETNAM

CO USAF HOSP, CLARK AB, P.I.

CONFID MAGAG-PO 667

Request determination as to type of projectile (gunshot, shrapnel, etc) that caused death of Maj Dale R. Buis, 0494655. Did projectile enter rear, front, right or left side of head. Were there any Wounds other than head wounds. If so, describe type of projectile and position of entry. ADMSG ASAP.

MAGAG-PO

E. L. QUILLIAN, Maj, AGC, Asst AG

WILLIAM C. DORN
Lt Col, AGC
Adjutant General

UNCLASSIFIED

PRIORITY
PRIORITY

0452Z 11 July 1959 [11:52 A.M. local]

CHMAAG VIETNAM

USAF HOSPITAL, CLARK AB

INFO: OQMG, WASH DC

UNCLAS MAGAG-PO 9658

Following message received from NOK of Major Dale R. Buis. Quote "Forward following from Mrs. Buis: Desires body be escorted to Fort Rosecrans Calif. for military funeral including graveside services. Request notifications ASAP on ETA of body. Requests personal effects be shipped to 91 East Emerson Street Chulavista, California." Unquote. Escort personnel have been selected to accompany remains of Major Buis and MSgt Chester M. Ovnand. If possible would prefer remains be accompanied from Clark. ADMSG ASAP ETD of remains.

E.L. Quillian, Maj, AGC, Asst AG

WILLIAM C. DORN,
Lt Col, AGC
Adjutant General

UNCLASSIFIED

PRIORITY

0454Z 11 July 1959 [11:54 A.M. local]

CHMAAG VIETNAM

CG FT MAC ARTHUR, CALIF

UNCLAS MAGAG-PO 9659 Pass to Col A. L. Leonard, Los Angeles, Calif.

Remains Maj Buis evacuated to Clark AB 8 July. Your message relayed there and to OQMC. Major James S. Hinkle selected as escort officer. Efforts being made to have Major Hinkle accompany remains from Clark. Will keep you advised.

E.L. Quillian, Maj, AGC, Asst AG

WILLIAM C. DORN,
Lt Col, AGC
Adjutant General

UNCLASSIFIED

PRIORITY

0456Z 11 July 1959 [11:56 A.M. local]

CHIEF, MAAG VIETNAM

SENIOR ADVISOR
5th MILITARY REGION
CAN THO, VIETNAM

SENIOR ADVISOR
I VN CORPS
DANANG, VIETNAM

UNCLAS MAGCG-CH 9660D

Tours Major Hinkle and Master Sergeant Becker curtailed. Orders being amended. Hinkle and Becker detailed as escorts of honor for movement of bodies two deceased MAAG personnel to CONUS, Planes arrive Danang 121030 July 1959 and at Can Tho 120845 July 1959. Two personnel concerned will be returned to Saigon for immediate processing and detailed instructions. Hinkle and Becker will not return to their duty stations after pick-up Sunday 12 July.

N/R: TMX alerts two MAAG personnel of tour curtailment for purpose of escorting to CONUS bodies of two MAAG personnel killed in 8 July incident.

JAMES A. GRIMBLEY, Lt Col,Inf
Exec Off, CATO Division

On 14 July 1959, Dale's wife, Virginia, wrote a letter to Dale's brother, James, and his wife Isabel:

> "Just rec'd the first news today . . . concerning Dale's return. He will arrive on or about 16 July Travis AFB, San Francisco. Captain Trimm from Rosecrans surmises Dale will arrive in San Diego on or about the 20th and services will be conducted on or about the 22nd or 23rd.
>
> "I have made arrangements for graveside services with full military honors to be held at Fort Rosecrans National Cemetery. There will be no chapel services. I believe this is the way Dale wants it. I am sure Dale would like you there and to know I would if you can so arrange. However, if not, we will both understand – distance and commitments some times makes our wishes a little difficult so if you can't don't feel badly.
>
> "No words can express my feelings as you must no doubt know. Thank heavens he has three fine sons of which he was tremendously proud of, and which are as proud of him.
>
> "My sympathy goes out to you and family. There's not more I can say.
>
> "Virginia"

Mrs. Ovnand received letters about the death of her husband from Washington and Vietnam. The U.S. Ambassador to Vietnam, Elbridge Durbrow, expressed sorrow. The President of South Vietnam, Ngo Dinh Diem, spoke of "the indignation of the populace on the subject of this latest outrage."

"We felt uncomfortable using the large dining table in the main building after having used it as a mortuary platform, so shortly after the attack we replaced it with two smaller tables – one a little larger than the other," recalled Victor Gorlinsky.

"Colonel Ellsworth Davis asked me to write the letter about Master Sergeant Ovnand to his wife who resided near Fort Hood. It was an honor for me to do this," said Victor Gorlinsky. "He was not only a good soldier, but a good friend."

MAAG Deputy Chief of Staff, Major General Engels, always sympathetic and friendly to his MAAG advisors, pitches horseshoes at the BIF Compound during an inspection break, several weeks after the 8 July 1959 attack. General Engels spent almost all his time in travel and regularly visited and inspected all units in the field to keep General "Hanging Sam" Williams informed, and to ensure uniformity in the Vietnamese training effort. Courtesy of LTC Victor W. Gorlinsky, US Army (ret.)

Chapter 13
Off Shore and Locked Down

U.S. Marines swarm down a cargo net as they train for a beach landing US Marine Corps photo

Even though only modest mention was given to the killings of Major Dale Buis and Master Sergeant Chester Ovnand in the stateside press, in secret, elements of the 3d Marine Division went on alert on the island of Okinawa. Some of those units actually deployed with the destination of Vietnam.

Corporal Edward Mayzel recalled, "Back in July 1959, I was a private First Class waiting for my promotion to Lance Corporal. The outfit I was with for thirteen months was the 3d Light Support

Company, 3d Service Battalion, 3d Marine Division. A light support company's job is to supply ammo, fuel, food, water purification, vehicles, weapons, ordnance, and casualty support for combat units. Our unit was attached to the second wave that was scheduled to land on a beach somewhere in Vietnam. The first wave left by aircraft from Kadena Air Base, while we loaded ships at Okinawa's White Beach day and night, and in a few days we were out to sea. The first wave of our group departed in more than half a dozen ocean going vessels and steamed to a location off the coast of Vietnam. Our company was separated and I was on an AKA, a flattop which carries vehicles. We were at sea at least ten days, possibly two weeks. We had our weapons, but were allowed no ammo while at sea. I asked about this and my sergeant told me that we would be issued ammunition just before we hit the beach."

In 1996, another Marine with the 3d Marine Division, Joe Atkinson, stated, "It's been over thirty years, but I do recall the time we were off the coast of Vietnam. We had been offshore of Southeast Asia before that, but the trip to Vietnam was because of the things happening there at the time – the deaths of the two U.S. Army advisors. It was not a pleasant voyage by any means. I remember looking out at other ships in the convoy and watched their props come plum out of the water. The ocean was rough – really rough."

The Task Force lay in the open sea just beyond the view of Vietnam's coastline. At night, domes of light radiated from coastal cities just beyond the horizon. "We could see the coast on occasion as we sat off shore, but we never made final preparations to land," said Atkinson. "I don't recollect how long we were out there, but finally we turned around and went back to home port."

Mayzel reflected, "I never did find out what happened to the first wave which had been flown in. The 2d Light Support Company was part of that force. When we got back to Okinawa, we remained on standby and thought that we might eventually be headed back to Vietnam, but they cut my orders stateside and I left in October 1959 for home. All the ships and bases on Okinawa were still on standby for Vietnam when I left. The alert was a direct result of the deaths of the two Americans."

DEPARTMENT OF THE NAVY
HEADQUARTERS UNITED STATES MARINE CORPS
MARINE CORPS HISTORICAL CENTER
WASHINGTON NAVY YARD
WASHINGTON, D.C. 20374-0580

IN REPLY REFER TO
5750/917
& 1297
HDH-2/LK
8 Aug 88

Mr. Edward M. Mayzel
144 Harvard Drive
Torrington, Connecticut 06790

Dear Mr. Mayzel:

This is in response to your recent requests for information on a 1959 Marine Corps operation.

Despite a detailed review of available unit files, reports, and daily diaries for the time period referenced in your letter, we were unable to locate information relating to the operation described in your letter. Unfortunately, reporting requirements for Marine Corps units between the Korean War and the Vietnam War were not stringent, and therefore, available records for that time period are limited. Hopefully, your request for information from your service record book will provide more information.

We regret that we were not able to be of more assistance to you.

Sincerely,

Robert V. Aquilina (for)

DANNY J. CRAWFORD
Head, Reference Section
History and Museums Division

In Edward Mayzel's 1988 quest for information regarding 1959 Marine Corps operations off the coast of Vietnam, the U.S. Marine Corps Historical Center could furnish little in detail. Courtesy of Edward Mayzel

It was later learned that the first wave of Marines that flew into Vietnam arrived at Bien Hoa Air Base and were locked down in hangars until the Task Force's alert status was finally called off. No mention of the ten-day wait at sea was ever officially made. While one anonymous report has come to light which states that

Marines actually landed in several aircraft at both Bien Hoa and Tan Son Nhut near Saigon. Upon arrival of those airplanes the Marines were marched into several large hangars where they stayed for many days. "We were not allowed to leave the hangars, no matter what our personal circumstances were," former U.S. Marine Kenneth Whick told me in April 1997. "We were locked down and while incommunicado we ate, crapped and slept in the hangars. We were never officially told that we were in Vietnam, or what was coming next. When I asked my platoon leader, 'What the Hell is going on sir?' He told me, 'You're a Marine make the most of it.'"

Chapter 14
Young Bai

Young Bai proudly poses with his new bicycle, which was purchased by members of MAAG 7. LTC Victor W. Gorlinsky, US Army (ret.)

After the attack on Bien Hoa, reports indicated that the little eight year old Vietnamese boy, the mess cook's son, had been killed by the Viet Cong.

"There was a little boy always hanging around the area," said Howard Boston. "The cook's son offered to shine boots and perform other houseboy tasks when he wasn't hanging around the mess hall helping his father. For a little kid, he worked pretty hard. He did his best to pick up English, but like every Vietnamese kid that came in contact with American soldiers during the war, he ended up learning more G.I. slang than anything else. His father, because he was the head cook, got paid more than the other Vietnamese working as K.P.s, but still only got a few dollars a day. The boy was often in the kitchen area, just off the mess hall.

It was learned, by one or more reporters, that the mess cook's eight-year-old son had been lying outside the mess hall on the ground wounded, which became more dramatic when changed to, "the mess cook's eight-year-old son, who had been watching the movie through a side window, lay dying." Another report stated, "The boy was hit by four slugs and died later." The supposition was carried forward for many years, and most all reports had the boy killed there at Bien Hoa along with Major Buis and Master Sergeant Ovnand.

"The boy was shot up pretty bad. They had him on a stretcher next to me when they enveloped my head in gauze," said Boston. "The Vietnamese medics were working on him when Vic and Beau transferred me to the U.S. Army Dispensary in Saigon. He was still alive when they took me out of the mobile medical center, and put me in the colonel's sedan."

The Vietnamese cooks quarters was located immediately to the left of the main building at MAAG 7 Courtesy of LTC Victor Gorlinsky, US Army (ret.)

"Young Bai," is the appropriate name for the youngster whose father was known as Mr. Bai. Howard Boston did not remember the boy's name, but when Vic Gorlinsky was asked the question, he remembered he was the son of Mr. Bai, the cook, and that the youngster lived with his family in the stucco shed, which was the cook's house, located immediately to the left of the main building. Mr. Bai, hired by the members of MAAG 7 in a private agreement, was paid out of the team's pooled separate-ration money to cook for them. Vic Gorlinsky would drive to the commissary in Saigon to pick up food and supplies, and as the mess officer, Vic had vivid memories of Mr. Bai.

Vic further explained that on the night of the attack Mr. Bai was no where to be found, therefore, one might think that he was complicit in the attack, or knew it was going to happen. However, it was learned he was picked up in Saigon for illegal gambling and thrown in jail where he spent a day or two. Mr. Bai would not have intentionally put his family in jeopardy leaving them at the BIF compound, or at least insuring that his son was not peering in the mess hall window at show-time. The reason for his absence and his non-involvement in the attack seems to hold water.

I did not know the boy was not killed until I spoke with Howard Boston in 1993, when I was told that at some point, he found himself lying on a stretcher near the youngster before he was evacuated to Saigon. When Boston explained that the boy had survived, it was then that I bombarded him with questions, figuring that other facts reported by the press may also have been incorrect, distorted, or misinterpreted.

As Young Bai, recovering from his chest wounds, was returned from a Vietnamese hospital, LTC Ellsworth Davis wanted to do something nice for the boy. The members of the advisory team decided to chip in and purchase the boy a bicycle. Yet the amicable arrangement between the Bai family and the advisors did not last. On the contrary it deteriorated. Mr. Bai's carousing and gambling continued to be a problem, meals were not prepared on time, and finally his employment was terminated. Mr. Bai, his wife, Young Bai, and the bicycle eventually moved off the BIF compound. The case in point is that the mess cook's eight year old son did not die in a hail of bullets as reported in the press.

The headquarters building of the 7th ARVN Infantry Division was located a mile from the BIF Compound. Photos courtesy of LTC Victor W. Gorlinsky, US Army (ret.)

The ARVN security building for the BIF Compound (foreground) and quarters of LTC Ellsworth Davis and Major Charles Watson (background).

Chapter 15
Boston Blackie Returns

Captain Howard Boston approaches an administrative building at the 7th ARVN Division compound, located adjacent to BIF. LTC Victor W. Gorlinsky, USA (ret.)

During the 8 July 1959 attack, Boston Blackie was wounded. Some reports said his wounds were "not serious." Some said "seriously wounded," while others stated, "critical."

"Right after the attack I was patched up by the Vietnamese," said Boston. "Of course, I was a little out of it so I'm not sure just where the initial medical attention happened, but I could see them treating the little Vietnamese boy next to me and recognized him as the mess cook's son. They gauzed my head up like a mummy's and I had just a little air hole in the dressing to breath. The Vietnamese were going to take me to Saigon by ambulance, but team members wanted to take me themselves. Vic and Beau walked me to the colonel's sedan. I could hear Beau in the front seat, but I'm not sure if he was driving. I know Vic cradled me in his arms in the back seat, and the conversation was, of course, about what had just happened. They tried to keep the fact that Sergeant Ovnand and Major Buis had been killed from me, but it was pretty evident. I couldn't talk, but tried to listen even with the ringing in my ear. I was uncomfortable but I felt like I was doing OK. When I got to the hospital they unwrapped my bandages. The doctor on duty checked my wound. He told me right then and there that I'd be evacuated in the morning."

CONFIDENTIAL

PRIORITY

1819Z 8 July 1959 [0119 hours local]

CHMAAG VIETNAM

TAG DA WASHDC

CONF MAGAG-CH _______ For AGPS.

Request you advise Mrs. Ardys Allene Boston, RFD 3, Blairsburg, Iowa of the following: Capt Howard B. Boston, Arty, wounded by gunshot from unidentified assailant when Advisor Detachment at Bien Hoa, Vietnam, was attacked at approximately 1900 hours, 8 July 1959. Condition not considered serious. Capt Boston now hospitalized MAAG Dispensary, Saigon, will be evacuated by air on 9 July to hospital at Clark AB, P.I. Downgraded to unclassified upon release by DA to NOK or news media.

WILLIAM C. DORN,
Lt Col, AGC
Adjutant General

"I received treatment at the hospital at Clark and was told that I'd be evacuated stateside, but it took almost two weeks to get me back to the states," Boston remembered.

The delay was not a medical one, nor was it about the unavailability of air transport. The problem was about Clark Air Base's public relations standing with the press. Medical considerations seemed to be taking a back seat. On 9 July 1959, shortly after Captain Boston's arrival at Clark Hospital, the U.S. press representatives in the Philippines got wind of the fact that Captain Boston had been evacuated there. Even though he was shot through the jaw and was barely able to talk, the press wanted interviews from him and Clark Air Base was eager to have Captain Boston tell the media how well he had been treated and cared for at their hospital. The media requested a press interview with the captain, which they formalized to the 13th Air Force, who liked the idea. Clark Air Base then put Captain Boston's transportation back to the states on hold "until he could be stabilized," while they contacted the Air Attaché Saigon, requesting interviews on behalf of the press. The Air Attaché contacted MAAG Vietnam requesting a Boston interview. That was when MAAG Vietnam Adjutant General LTC William C. Dorn contacted CINCPAC (Commander in Chief Pacific Command) in Hawaii in a "Confidential" Priority message:

> "Hq 13th AF has requested clearance through Air Attaché Saigon for press interview with Capt Howard B. Boston, US Army, wounded at Bien Hoa and evacuated this date to Clark Air Base Hospital. Request advise when clearance for such interview may be granted"

A copy of the CINCPAC response was not available, and Howard Boston remembered little about interviews at Clark Air Base. Boston finally arrived at Walter Reed on 25 July 1959, after spending sixteen days at Clark so that his jaw would heal enough to talk to the press.

"Once I got to Walter Reed Army Hospital they gave me a 003 MOS - that of patient. I stayed at Walter Reed about a month, then went back home to Iowa . . ."

From right to left - Howard Boston, his wife, Ardys, and their son, Robert, upon Robert's graduation from ROTC at Loras Academy in 1957. Two years later, Howard's visit home, after being released from Walter Reed, would not last long before he returned to Vietnam. Courtesy of Robert Boston

Boston Blackie was a popular fictional character in numerous movies from the 1920's through the late 1940's. Some Boston Blackie titles which applied to Howard Boston included *A Close Call for Boston Blackie,* in 1946, and the 1927 silent film *The Return of Boston Blackie.* These stand out because Boston Blackie's real life equivalent – Howard B. Boston, after having a close call of being shot through the face, and being patched up stateside, chose to return to Vietnam.

"A few months after he was evacuated we were told that Captain Boston requested he be returned to our detachment to complete his Vietnam tour," said Victor Gorlinsky.

"I had arrived in Vietnam in May 1959 and only had two months in country when I was shot," Howard explained. "I was only thirty-seven years old and other than the numbness in my face and the loss of hearing in my right ear, I was in good physical shape. There was no reason not to go back. I insisted that I be returned. I still had ten months to go."

> "**SAIGON, Vietnam, Oct 3, 1959 (UPI)** Capt. Howard B. Boston of Webster City, Iowa, returned to South Vietnam to-day, recovered from wounds received in a terrorist attack."

"It was a big event when Howard stepped off the Pan American Boeing Stratocruiser at Tan Son Nhut," remembered Vic. "The Vietnamese had a band playing and Colonel Cao, other officers and most of the detachment personnel from MAAG 7 were there to greet him."

Boston said, "I returned to my same room at the BIF Compound. One night after I got back, while I was shaving, the damned plaster came clear off the bathroom ceiling! It scared the Hell out of me!"

Boston's insistence to return is the kind of attitude which sets brave men apart from fictional characters. Heroism is not about being stupid fearless. It is about having doubts and fears and overcoming them. It is about hoping for the best and being ready for the worst.

Captains Howard Boston and Victor Gorlinsky still had a court-room adventure ahead of them.

GENERAL ORDERS No. 24

HEADQUARTERS, DEPARTMENT OF THE ARMY
WASHINGTON 25, D.C., *7 May 1962*

I.—PURPLE HEART. By direction of the President, under the provisions of Executive Order 11016, 25 April 1962, the Purple Heart for wounds received in action on the dates and locations indicated was awarded by the Department of the Army to the following named individuals:

Major *Howard B. Boston*, O955149, 8 July 1959, Vietnam
Specialist Five *Robert H. Bramlett*, RA24907146, 28 April 1962, Laos
Major *John Cevaal*, O2024518, 22 October 1957, Vietnam
Sergeant First Class *Charles G. Grant*, RO19575083, 22 October 1957, Vietnam
Master Sergeant *Frank E. Kent*, RA32075631, 22 October 1957, Vietnam
Master Sergeant *Charles E. Kille*, RA15078996, 22 October 1957, Vietnam
Master Sergeant *Charles G. McQuay*, RA20340764, 22 October 1957, Vietnam
Sergeant First Class *Nelson R. Moore*, RA26376409, 6 October 1961, Laos
Captain *Edward W. Nidever*, O72176, 28 October 1961, Vietnam
Major *Elsworth Reiss*, O1579006, 22 October 1957, Vietnam
Specialist Three *Theodoria Rosario-Mendez*, RA10407400, 22 October 1957, Vietnam
Specialist Four *Donald A. Ruths*, RA55410871, 22 October 1957, Vietnam
Captain *David C. Womack*, O2041141, 22 October 1957, Vietnam

II.—PURPLE HEART. By direction of the President, under the provisions of Executive Order 11016, 25 April 1962, the Purple Heart was awarded posthumously by the Department of the Army to the following named individuals who were killed in action on the dates and locations indicated:

Major *Dale R. Buis*, O494655, 8 July 1959, Vietnam
Specialist Four *James T. Davis*, RA14696877, 22 December 1961, Vietnam
Specialist Five *James Gabriel, Jr.*, RA10110424, 8 April 1962, Vietnam
Lieutenant Colonel *Frank W. Lynn*, O26448, 3 September 1954, Kinman Island
Staff Sergeant *Wayne E. Marchand*, RA27710818, 8 April 1962, Vietnam
Lieutenant Colonel *Alfred Mendendorp*, O336197, 3 September 1954, Kinman Island
Master Sergeant *Chester M. Ovnand*, RA36243358, 8 July 1959, Vietnam

Warrant Officer *Edgar W. Weitkamp, Jr.*, W2211566, 23 March 1961, Laos

[AG 200.6 (4 May 62)]

BY ORDER OF THE SECRETARY OF THE ARMY:

G. H. DECKER,
General, United States Army,
Chief of Staff.

Official:
J. C. LAMBERT,
Major General, United States Army,
The Adjutant General.

Distribution:
To be distributed in accordance with DA Form 12–4 requirements.

It was not until the tenure of MAAG Commander Lieutenant General Lionel C. McGarr that orders authorizing Purple Hearts for those wounded and killed in Vietnam were issued. The first name was Howard Boston. Courtesy of Bruce Swander

Chapter 16
The Bien Hoa Seven

After the attack on Bien Hoa, the BIF Compound was often the scene of extra security. Here ARVN Security Forces remain seated in jeeps awaiting instructions.

Courtesy of LTC Victor W. Gorlinsky, US Army (ret.)

The behavior of the Viet Cong cell operating from an island on the Dong Nai River was described by South Vietnamese officials as an aggressive criminal act, rather than any kind of military operation against foreign intruders as the Viet Cong would have the local populace believe. After the capture of some of the VC raiders there was the "public notion," advanced by the Diem government, of a legal proceeding to deal with the terrorists, something that the U.S. and South Vietnamese news media could cover, or, at least, make mention of in stateside press reports.

On 9 December 1959, a Vietnamese prosecutor requested that Captain Boston and Captain Gorlinsky go to the Bien Hoa Security

Police Station. The prosecutor's objective was to verify events that took place during the attack. The question and answer period and the discussion that followed were informal. The prosecutor then asked the two officers if they would appear as witnesses at a trial of the seven apprehended Viet Cong agents, to be held at a later date. The two officers explained that they would have to withhold their answer to participate in any courtroom proceedings, pending approval from the Chief of MAAG Lieutenant General Samuel T. Williams. After the question was again asked through channels, and MAAG gave approval for the two to testify, the captains were notified to appear at the Bien Hoa city courthouse at 0730 hours, 29 December 1959.

During the court session, Howard Boston and Victor Gorlinsky were permitted to sit in the courtroom, and through an interpreter they were able to follow the trial. After the proceedings Captain Gorlinsky submitted a brief narrative concerning the special military court. The seven accused Viet Cong were present and the court reporter read the charges and events surrounding the case and named the accused and witnesses who were to appear. The seven accused stood before the court president and each was identified, then the witnesses had their turn. Unfortunately, Vic Gorlinsky did not get every name.

During the morning session each accused was questioned by members of the court, then cross examined by the court prosecutor. Lawyers for the accused did very little during this opening part of the session. All evidence and the investigation reports were in the hands of the court president. It appeared that the morning hearings were for the purpose of making the trial public, little or nothing in new or recently disclosed material was added that did not appear in documentation. The court president excused the two American witnesses at 1130 hours, after four or five of the accused had appeared before him. Vic and Howard were told to return at 1445 hours for the afternoon session which actually started at 1500 hours.

"The trial was in no way dramatic," said Vic. The drama was yet to come.

Outside the courtroom there was interest and curiosity among the local population. The crowd was mostly interested in the media event occurring in their town, which in 1959 was still a tranquil little village.

"Everything went off well. It appeared that the main purpose for Captain Boston and I appearing as witnesses, was to verify that an incident did take place and to establish facts concerning it," remembered Vic. "Major Hallett had already rotated back to the states, and I never saw Colonel Clay again. It seemed that MAAG had tried to keep his name out of any information released about the attack right from the start. During the court procedure, there was no swearing in or affirming of persons appearing before the court. They simply stood up and testified."

Captain Howard Boston (left) and Captain Victor Gorlinsky (right) were the only two officers that testified at the trial of the communist raiders. LTC Victor W. Gorlinsky, USA (ret.)

Based on some of the testimony, it appeared that orders for a "test raid" on an American installation and/or American personnel were developed in Zone D at a quarterly meeting of VC leaders during April 1959, although no mention was given as to Hanoi's involvement. Later during May, it was decided that raids would take place in Bien Hoa Province. This information was given to the court by a communist known as Nguyen Van Hoa, who was the Viet Cong cell leader in the Province of Bien Hoa. He lived near the BIF Compound in the village of Tam Hiep. Statements from the others accused, as well as testimony of witnesses, indicated that the Viet Cong had a fairly extensive organization in Bien Hoa Province. Frequent VC meetings were held, dues and taxes were regularly collected, and plans of terror were developed. Hoa stated that the raid on Bien Hoa was finalized during May 1959, and according to him, he was not certain of the details whether the raid was to be an ambush along the road or as an attack on the BIF Compound. Hoa did indicate that the raid would be made somewhere between the new highway at Tam Hiep and Bien Hoa City. Although he did not address the subject, his instructions came from further up his chain of command.

The leader of the attacking party, appointed as such for diversion purposes, confessed to his participation and told how they used his sampan, plus one other boat, to move on the river to an area near the BIF Compound.

In all, there were seven men accused: (1) Nguyen Van Hoa, the Viet Cong cadre chief for Bien Hoa Province; (2) The supposed leader of the raid and boatman, who was actually not much more than a guide who knew the river well; (3) Another participant in the raid who had been armed and was involved in the actual shooting; (4) A resident of Tam Hiep and a staunch member of the Communist Party who gave food and shelter to members of the raiding party, but who never admitted to the fact that he had harbored at least two North Vietnamese soldiers in his home; (5) A terrorist, who was described simply as "a clerk in the Bien Hoa Viet Cong"; (6) Another admitted communist who also gave food and shelter to the raiding party; and finally (7) the second boatman.

In addition to witnesses Boston and Gorlinsky, there were seven Vietnamese who testified. They included: (1) a woman living on Dong Nai Island who allowed her house to be used as a rendezvous point for Viet Cong; (2) another woman, described as the wife of "a dead Viet Cong agent," approached by members of the raiding party for food and assistance after the raid. Probably, the wife of the sapper who had been killed by the satchel-charge; and (3) a young boy who helped the Viet Cong, although how he helped was never really revealed. The testimony of the other four witnesses who were called was vague. (4 & 5) There were two old women who had relatives that had been identified as Viet Cong, however, the women said they knew nothing; (6) a boy from the BIF Compound who was near the mess hall when the raid took place (this was not Young Bai); and finally, (7) another Vietnamese whose testimony was brief and shed no new light on what had happened.

A boat beached on the Dong Nai River and curious children on the riverbank
LTC Victor W. Gorlinsky, USA (ret.)

The operator of the second boat, an unwilling participant, was forced to transport half of the attacking party and waited with the boats. It was revealed that the second boatman knew two of the raiders who lived on Dong Nai Island, and through him the two men were identified and apprehended by security forces.

In summary, the court's prosecutor stated the first apprehension was made on 28 July, only twenty days after the attack, and vigorous effort had been made to bring the accused men to trial without delay. He mentioned these Viet Cong had been living on an island on the Dong Nai River, not far from the compound, and informants loyal to the South Vietnamese government had turned them in.

He asked the court to be impartial and to arrive at verdicts based on the facts of the testimony. He, further, stated that international eyes were on this particular court, and a fair and thorough trial would prove to the rest of the world that the Republic of Vietnam was taking prompt and effective measures against the communist threat. It is of interest to note that there was no mention, at anytime during the trial, of the death's of the two Vietnamese soldiers or the wounding of the Vietnamese mess cook's son. Only the deaths of Dale Buis, Chester Ovnand, and the wounding of Howard Boston were spotlighted.

"The comments I have related here concerning the trial were gained through an interpreter and Captain Phuong of the Chief of Province Office Bien Hoa. They are by no means complete," said Vic Gorlinsky. "The trial went off quickly, therefore, being in Vietnamese it was not possible to get complete details. At 1500 hours, the court opened again and Captain Boston was the first witness called. He was asked to give the court a statement as to what happened on the night of 8 July 1959. I was the next witness and was asked to relate, in my own words, the events of the night as I knew them. My testimony at this time was substantially the same as the original statement made to Colonel Symroski at the Brink BOQ on the night of 8 July 1959. There was no cross examination; however, the defense attorney objected to the presence of Captain Boston and myself in the courtroom. The Court President overruled him. The remaining witnesses appeared and confirmed statements made earlier, and in some instances pointed out certain of those who had been accused.

"After all the witnesses were called, the three defense attorneys made pleas for those accused. Each spoke about thirty minutes on behalf of his respective client or clients. On conclusion of the pleas, each accused was given an opportunity to make a final statement."

Howard Boston said, "At the end of the trial, four of the seven accused were given the death penalty and scheduled for execution. Three got prison sentences. The Vietnamese wanted to execute the four at the BIF Compound because the South Vietnamese normally performed public executions at the scene of a crime, but the compound was U.S leased property and MAAG wouldn't have it."

Existing records identifying the four to be executed are vague and only Nguyen Van Hoa is mentioned by name. The four were: (1) Hoa, the Viet Cong cadre leader; (2) another man who was designated the leader of the raiding party who was also a boatman; (3) a third participant in the raid unidentified by name; and (4) the individual identified only as a Viet Cong "clerk" who participated in the attack, and who had been privy to plans and records.

Boston explained, "During the trial they scheduled the four to be executed by firing squad across the road from the BIF Compound."

On their execution date the four Viet Cong, with their hands bound behind their backs, were dragged out of two vehicles which had pulled-up across the road from the BIF Compound entrance. South Vietnamese soldiers armed with M1 carbines exited a third truck. The four convicted men were placed against a brick wall to prevent stray bullet injury of any by-standers. The men were not offered blind folds. They were given a command to look in the direction of the BIF compound where their crimes had been committed. As the command to lock and load was given to the firing squad, one man opened his mouth wide and gave out a wail that could be heard across the road. It sounded like it would never stop. Another man crumbled to his knees in despair, while a third prisoner urinated involuntarily in anticipation of the command to fire being given. Only one man stood firm – frozen in fear. Moments later there was the crack of eight rifles being fired in rapid succession as twenty-four rounds hit their marks. Chunks of Vietnamese brick and blood exploded in the target area. The four men hit the wall and then crumbled to the ground.

Because the attack on Bien Hoa, for political reasons, was regarded as an act of murder and not an act of war, the Department of Defense has yet to recognize that the Vietnam War began on 8 July 1959 with the attack on, and deaths of, Major Dale R. Buis and Master Sergeant Chester M. Ovnand, and the execution of their attackers.

Chapter 17
The Ngoc Hanh/Hon-Dai Hypothesis

Since 1959, North Vietnamese soldiers infiltrated into South Vietnam down a series of trails through North Vietnam, Laos and Cambodia. US Army Carlisle Barracks, PA

Only four of the attackers who had entered the BIF Compound at Bien Hoa had been found guilty of a capital crime and executed. Most all accounts put, at least, six terrorists at the attack, not including one of the boatman who stayed with the boats at the river bank. There are only incomplete records of the trial and execution, and even more obscure was the probability that covert agents from North Vietnam were involved in the attack as General Sam Williams, specifically, mentioned to his National Archives interviewer at the Lyndon Baines Johnson Library on 16 March 1981.

Was Williams' assessment of that aspect of the attack viable? Even with (1) Nguyen Van Hoa, the VC cadre leader; (2) another man appointed in charge of the raiding party; (3) the man who was identified as a third participant in the raid; and (4) the VC clerk, all executed, this still meant that at least two other killers never stood trial. Who were these other two men and what happened to them?

Originally, those in Hanoi in charge of the infiltration effort, tasked by Ho Chi Minh to send terrorists south, sought to fill their quotas with soldiers and others born in South Vietnam. The 90,000 troops that moved from South Vietnam to the North, after the Geneva Accords ended the Indochina War in 1954, provided an invaluable reservoir of men for this purpose.

Beginning in 1959, communist soldiers and technicians reentered South Vietnam under orders from Hanoi. From 1959 to 1960, when Hanoi was establishing its infiltration pipeline, at least 1,800 men moved into South Vietnam from the North that first year (1959-1960). They were ordered into the South through adjoining Laos and Cambodia remaining under military discipline of the high command in Hanoi. Special training camps operated by the North Vietnamese Army gave political and military training to these soon-to-be infiltrators, while special infiltration units were responsible for moving men from North Vietnam into the South via infiltration trails through Laos.

A typical infiltrator (we'll call *Ngoc-Hanh*) was born in South Vietnam sometime in the 1930's. He went through five to seven years of school and then worked on his parent's farm. During the war against the French, he joined Viet Minh forces. When the fighting ended with the defeat of the French at Dien Bien Phu, he was transferred to North Vietnam with his unit. He remained in the North Vietnamese Army until the mid to late 1950's, when he was sent to work on a state farm with thousands of other men and women. In the late 1950's, he was told he must join a newly activated NVA battalion, of which all of its members came from provinces in South Vietnam. It was not an ordinary battalion; half or even more of its members were cadre with ranks up to senior captain.

Such battalions went to special training camps, and were put through advanced training courses that lasted six months in preparation for fighting alongside Viet Cong already in South Vietnam. These training programs included combat tactics for units from squad to company, and techniques of guerilla tactics and counter-guerilla fighting. Three fourths of the training was military including terrorist techniques, ambushes, and sabotage, while one fourth included heavy doses of political indoctrination, with much emphasis on the necessity for armed power against the South.

The second infiltrator (we'll call *Hon-Dai*), was most likely a VC weapons or explosives technician, about thirty years old and a native of the greater Saigon area. He may have joined the Viet Minh in the 1950's. After three years of military service he may have been assigned to a military farm, and later worked in a secret arsenal manufacturing weapons for use by guerrilla forces. Like *Ngoc-Hanh,* he went to North Vietnam after the Geneva Accords were signed in 1954. In North Vietnam, *Hon-Dai* attended a technical school specializing in arms manufacture. He received special training in some small arms and artillery. At the end of 1958, he was ordered to attend a special course of political training in preparation for infiltrating into South Vietnam. Upon completion of the training course, he was assigned to a group of about fourteen men who would move south together.

In early 1959, both *Ngoc-Hanh* and *Hon-Dai* received orders to move south with their battalions and followed the same route. They were transported in trucks from deep in North Vietnam to provinces just north of the 17th parallel, then their units were moved westward to the Lao border. Along with more than 300 men, they began walking south following mountain trails in Laos and the Vietnam border area. They marched by day and rested by night. Every fifth day they stopped at a way-station for a full day's rest. Companies would drop off along the trail, for example, first at Thua Thien Province, then another group at Pleiku Province, four border provinces later. As the group thinned out it was realized that *Ngoc-Hanh* and *Hon-Dai* would become part of the same terrorist appendage. While the team headed for Bien Hoa after weeks of marching, they crossed over into Cambodia and finally Vietnam's Phuoc Long Province. Their journey down the Ho Chi Minh Trail lasted slightly over five months.

Nguyen Van Hoa, the Bien Hoa communist cell chief, was a deep cover plant, instructed to remain in the south while most communists had moved north in 1954. Five years later, in May 1959, he was contacted by the small cell of communist infiltrators.

Typically, infiltrators made plans with chiefs like Hoa, to recruit local youth for service with the Viet Cong, to round up cattle and rice, and to kill or kidnap village chiefs, priests, nuns, and teachers, but, most importantly, in this new phase, the program was to kill members of the U.S. military stationed in South Vietnam. When contact was made, *Ngoc-Hanh* and *Hon-Dai* used false names, even to their fellow communists, giving them only the information immediately needed that American advisors at Bien Hoa would be attacked once plans were finalized. *Ngoc-Hanh* and *Hon-Dai* were kept undercover, hidden and given food and shelter by a man who lived in the nearby village of Tam Hiep. They limited their activities mainly to Dong Nai Island, occasionally reconning the American advisory compound at Bien Hoa, and watching the Americans water ski passed their island with their power boat.

Immediately after the attack, the two North Vietnamese communist agents disappeared, changing their identities and going to their family's homes elsewhere in the greater Saigon area – most likely south of the city, well away from Bien Hoa. They had been selected because of their knowledge of the Saigon area, because of their dialects, and the fact that they could disappear after the attack, away from where it had happened. Their allies in the attack had been sworn to secrecy about their existence. In 1959, it was "Top Secret" information that the North Vietnamese were engineering attacks in the south. If the locals were caught and were found out, they could face execution as they ultimately did. However, if the locals had divulged North Vietnam involvement in the attack, not only would they be tortured and killed, but their families would have been as well. *Ngoc-Hanh* and *Hon-Dai* were never found because their very existence was never acknowledged. Thus, the real perpetrators of the attack on Bien Hoa were never brought to justice. Like everything else that transpired in South Vietnam, nothing was about truth, but only the semblance of truth, and moreover nothing was about justice, but only the semblance of justice. While in the North, everything that transpired was based upon lies, propaganda and communist power "for the good of the people". While specially trained North Vietnamese agents were sent south to recruit, steal, murder, and maim, Ho Chi Minh conducted his *Song of Solidarity* across a country he had no rights to.

Chapter 18
The Aftermath

Ho Chi Minh conducts an orchestra performing "Song of Solidarity" in Hanoi on 3 September 1960, during a time he was sending young men from North Vietnam down trails to fight and die in the South Author's collection

The trial and executions at Bien Hoa deterred absolutely nothing when it came to communist terrorism directed against the south.

In July, the Lao Dong (Worker's Party of Vietnam) of which Ho Chi Minh became Secretary-General in 1956, had organized Group 759 to study ways to ship men and supplies to South Vietnam by both land and sea. The activities of Group 759 and a second group, Group 559, were kept highly secret because they were in clear violation of the Geneva agreements. Their purpose was a single-minded one, to illegally transport Viet Cong "paramilitary" units into South Vietnam to create terror among the population there.

In North Vietnam, Ho Chi Minh launched a brutal campaign of armed attacks, directed and controlled by his military underlings, against helpless civilians in the south, which were supported by international communism.

Incredibly, while he directed young men and women of North Vietnam to leave their homes and journey down the series of trails that would bear his name, "Gentle Uncle Ho" furthered his own kindly image, by participating in activities such as conducting North Vietnam's National Orchestra in concert. By 1960, an estimated four-thousand-five-hundred infiltrators illegally migrated south - their sole purpose; to create terror in South Vietnam.

In December 1960, a report to the International Control Commission revealed that during that year the Viet Cong had destroyed or damaged 284 bridges, burned 60 medical aid stations, and destroyed so many classrooms that some 25,000 children were deprived of schooling. The communists targeted local governments, public transportation and other essential services.

From 18 to 24 October 1961, General Maxwell Taylor visited South Vietnam, and learned of the state of emergency declared by President Ngo Dinh Diem because of a two-fold problem. First, because of severe flooding in the Mekong Delta after heavy monsoon rains, and secondly because of increased Viet Cong activity directed against the people of South Vietnam. Within a month, President John F. Kennedy dispatched two U.S. Army CH-21 helicopter companies to Vietnam - the 8th Transportation Company from Fort Bragg, North Carolina, and the 57th Transportation Company from Fort Lewis, Washington. The mission of the two companies was to provide ARVN soldiers with a means to control isolated areas flying them into combat to quell Viet Cong attacks. Within days after the arrival of the two units in Vietnam, on 22 December 1961, U.S. Army SP4 James T. Davis, assigned to the 509th Army Security Agency (ASA) was killed during a search for a Viet Cong radio transmitter when Davis and Vietnamese soldiers, unknowingly, drove into a Viet Cong ambush on Provincial Highway 10 near Duc Hoa.

As U.S. advisors increased in number, the BIF Compound underwent some significant changes. The 5th ARVN Division moved from Song Mao to Bien Hoa, while the designations MAAG 5 and MAAG 7 were sent north to I Corps near the DMZ. The advisory team at Bien Hoa then became MAAG Team 98 and the MAAG Team at Song Mao became MAAG Team 37.

The entrance to the Train Compound with Boston and Hallett's former quarters seen through the archway. I. Johnson

In 1962, another enemy attack brought about a name change for the BIF Compound. On 16 June, U.S. Army officers 1LT William F. Train III and Captain Walter R. McCarthy were riding in an open jeep near Ben Cat, as the third vehicle in a seven vehicle convoy, when it was ambushed and both were killed. On 8 June 1963, MAAG Vietnam General Orders Number 52, designated the BIF Compound as the Train Compound in honor of Lieutenant Train. By then a new building had been built behind the old main building (Building 57), where the 1959 attack had occurred. The building housed a new mess hall, chapel, a movie theatre, and a library. Building 57 (with new green shutters) then became the headquarters and administrative offices for the MAAG detachment.

After the take over by the communists in 1975, most of the buildings on the Train Compound were destroyed with the exception of the main building, known as Building 57. Photos by Mickey Speck

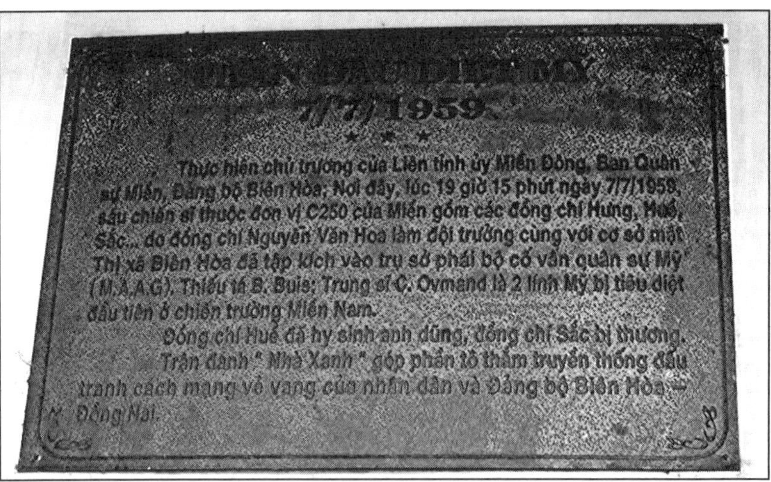

Although some of the information inscribed on the plaque, placed in the main building by the communists, is not accurate it reads:

The First Engagement to Destroy Americans
7 July 1959

Following orders to fight in Bien Hoa Province in the Eastern Military Region by the Communist Committee at 1915 hours on 7 July 1959 - six soldiers of the C 250 unit of the region - comrades Hung, Hue, Sac [and others] led by Nguyen Van Hoa, Platoon Chief of the Secret Office at Bien Hoa organized and engaged an attack against American MAAG advisors, Major B. Buis and Sergeant C. Ovmand who were killed in the first battle of South Vietnam. Comrade Hue sacrificed his life. Comrade Sac was wounded. The "Battle of the Green House" fighting was to prove the determination of the United Revolution of the Bien Hoa/Dong Nai Communist Party. Photo by Mickey Speck; Translation by David Do

Chapter 19
Still Part of the Family

Major Dale Buis and CWO Mitsugi Kasai at the U.S. Army Language School in 1958
Photo courtesy of CW4 Mitsugi Kasai, USA (ret)

In 1978, Dale Buis' wife, Virginia, wrote a letter to Dale's niece, Gretchen Buis, the Buis family historian, about memories of her husband and the best of times she had spent with him in Occupied Japan. "Two years doesn't seem like very long – but when it embraces every day of those two years – it can be a lifetime," she wrote. "In reflecting back, I think Dale was very complex – he was fun loving; serious about his military side; and had a good father image... he was a good father because he loved children – he really understood children – and he was very proud of his sons! Yet, Dale's responsibility was to his career – as it should be with men."

Virginia explained, "He was credited with saving the lives of the rest (of those at the movie) and they named a Bachelor Officers Quarters in Cholon after him. The BOQ became an intelligence center."

On 16 May 1962, after President John F. Kennedy issued Executive Order 11016, 25 April 1962, and after General Orders No. 24, dated 7 May 1962 authorized Major Dale Buis a posthumous Purple Heart, 11-year-old Kurt Buis was presented the award at Fort MacArthur, California, by Brigadier General C. de W. W. Lane. During that ceremony, General Lane told Kurt, "Remember your father always. He is an ideal to live by."

When Virginia wrote to Gretchen, she said that after his father's death, Kurt made a trip back to Pender, Nebraska, to spend time there. "One of the reasons Kurt made the trip...was because I wanted him to know and remember and have a pleasant feeling about the side of the family he might never have known otherwise.

"All three of the boys are definitely Buis'. They have Dale's looks, his mannerisms – which is really spooky at times. Kurt was helping me put in a flower bed the other day and turned to say something and I just stood rooted to the ground – he spoke and looked just like his father. Same mannerisms – and then darn if he didn't turn and walk over to the hose holding up his arms like Dale used to do. I finally laughed and told him and he just grinned."

"Kurt finished his masters in clinical psychology," wrote his mother, "and is opting for a position with the Board of Education, in the meantime he has been counseling at Breen Elementary. He, like his father, is best with pre-teen children. He can get them to do things that the rest could never get done."

Virginia Buis would often tell Kurt and the other two boys, Lance and Mark, about the times she and their father had when the couple had first met in Japan, and how after Dale returned from Korea, Mark was thirteen months old and Kurt was nearly three when his family finally caught up with Dale in Sendai, Japan...A year later, Lance came along ."

Not knowing a lot about her husband's actual military training, or his experiences in combat, Virginia characterized Dale simply as "A true soldier-of-fortune at heart."

In an 8 July 1984 interview with *Houston Post* staff reporter, Richard Rothschild, Kurt Buis said,

> "We never made a big thing about my father being the first, just the fact that, with the building of the Vietnam Veterans Memorial, the country finally had gotten to recognize the returning veterans."

In her 1978 letter, Virginia Buis wrote about Dale's funeral, "Services at Rosecrans National Cemetery were military, there was only a service at the gravesite with a very large gathering, the buglers and his flag-draped coffin. The site is part of Point Loma that stretches out to sea. I seldom go over there anymore, but can look over at the point and know where he is . . ."

Virginia Buis died of heart failure in 1983. She was preceded by her two youngest sons Mark and Lance.

There is not much on file at the National Personnel Records Center in St. Louis, Missouri, as far as Major Dale R. Buis' military service goes. On 12 July 1973, a fire destroyed the major portion of records of Army personnel who served from the period 1912 through 1959, and even though there are alternate record sources that often contain information which can be used to reconstruct some service record data lost in that fire, complete records cannot be reconstructed. The records center is aware that Dale Buis was awarded the American Campaign Medal, the Asiatic Pacific Campaign Medal with two bronze service stars, the Philippine Liberation Medal, the World War II Victory Medal and the Combat Infantryman's Badge. They have no record that he received the Bronze Star, the Army Commendation Medal, the United Nations Medal, the Korea Service Medal, or a posthumous Purple Heart. Regardless of any discrepancies concerning the Buis records, his name will stand and endure as the first name on the Vietnam Veterans Memorial located immediately below the date 1959.

Capt. Dale R. Buis (left), son of Mrs. Serena K. Buis, of 5104 Cuming street, receives a Commendation Ribbon from Col. Lloyd Moses, XVI Corps' chief of staff, at a ceremony in Japan, for distinguished service in Eighth Army intelligence service in Korea. A veteran of 11 years, Capt. Buis also wears the Bronze Star medal, American Theatre Campaign Medal, Asiatic-Pacific Theatre medal, Philippines liberation medal, World War II victory medal and the LN and Korean service ribbons. His wife, Virginia, lives in Oakland, California.

This post Korean War news clipping, released by the public information office, XVI Corps lists the decorations awarded to Dale Buis, with the exception of the fact that LN is a spelling error which should have read UN indicating United Nations Ribbon for his Korean Service. Courtesy of Hon. J. Stephen Buis

Chapter 20
Preserving Memories

Chester M. Ovnand, US Army, stands behind the headquarters building at Fort Sheridan, Illinois, in 1951. Courtesy of John Sheridan

Chester Ovnand's wife Mildred was born in Topeka, Kansas, to Calvin and Cora Streeter, on 24 October 1907. "Millie" was raised in Chickasaw and El Reno, Oklahoma, graduating from El Reno High School and majored in journalism at the University of Oklahoma at Norman. She only lacked a half a year to get her degree when she patriotically decided to take a hiatus and do something for her country during the years of World War II.

In 1944, Chet Ovnand was 30 and Millie was 37 when they met at the Camp Howze Service Club, Killeen, Texas, where she was the director. Before he left for the Pacific, Chet asked her to marry him, however, that would not happen immediately. It would not be until 26 February 1947, when Chet would begin calling Millie "Mrs. O".

"He was in the Pacific, island hopping for much of the war," said Millie. "New Guinea, Manila, and other of the smaller atolls. He was wounded and evacuated to the Philippines. Then, before Chet was released from assignment to the hospital in Manila, he had a jeep accident which prolonged his medical care. He came back to San Francisco on February 14, 1947, and we were married twelve days later on the 26th in the post chapel at Fort Bliss [Texas]. He had to have plastic surgery at William Beaumont Army Hospital for wounds he received in the Pacific, so we honeymooned in the army hospital where he stayed until August 1947. I visited him every chance I could. We played a lot of Gin Rummy as I sat at his bed-side. By the time he was released from Beaumont, I owed him $23,000 which I lost playing cards."

"After his assignments to places like Killeen Base, Texas; Austria, Panama, Korea, and Fort Sheridan, Illinois, he had served sixteen years in the Army when he chose Vietnam. He went there because he wanted to go, and again took up a position as first sergeant in a unit that consisted only of officers which didn't bother him at all, but he didn't like the climate in Southeast Asia," said Millie. "When he got there, he changed his mind and regretted going. He didn't write to me even once that there was any danger. He just wrote about the heat and the humidity and I knew that when he came back from Vietnam we'd be going to Alaska."

Several years after Chet's death, Millie Ovnand quit work at the Killeen Service Club in April 1968, when her eyes began giving her trouble. "Chet's death did something to my nerves, the calls and, then, the telegram I got later. I've never recovered."

In May 1972, speaking in a mild manner, Millie said, "They got their reporting all wrong, the reporter from the *Cleveland Plain Dealer* said Captain Boston told him Chet was shot in the abdomen and the throat, but that he managed to go upstairs and flip on the outside lights to light up the perimeter before he died there in the building."

Chester Ovnand's gravestone at Memorial Park Cemetery, Oklahoma City, Oklahoma
Photo courtesy of David Mitchell

The plaque at Ovnand Boulevard, Fort Hood, Texas
Photo courtesy of John Sheridan

It had taken thirteen years for Mildred Ovnand to learn of her husband's heroism. Previously, she had believed the press reports which stated he had died instantly.

Chester Ovnand was buried at Memorial Park Cemetery, Oklahoma City. Millie never remarried and when asked why, her reason was, "I know I can't find a twin to Chet."

Mildred Ovnand passed away at her home in December 1987. Growing up she was close to her cousin, William Bernard Sheridan, who served in Marrakech, Morocco, as a Morse code radio operator on Army Air Corps transports during World War II. Because she and Chester had no children, Mildred's estate went to William, who had two sons and two daughters. One of those sons, John Sheridan, as a boy was always fascinated with the fact that his Uncle Chet was "the first soldier to lose his life during the Vietnam War." M/Sgt Ovnand had died first, Major Dale Buis second, although their names are reversed on the Vietnam Veterans Memorial because of alphabetical format. When William passed away in 1989, John inherited Chester Ovnand's awards, his dog tags, a few photographs, and information about his military service which John guards with deep respect for his uncle. "I always was fascinated by Chester being the first," said John. "I asked for and received his items when my Dad passed in 1989. John Sheridan has been a great contributor to this work.

Chapter 21
Looking Back

Six months after the attack on Bien Hoa, senior advisors met in Saigon. (6) General Samuel T. Williams, Chief MAAG; (7) Colonel Charles Symroski, MAAG Chief Intelligence Officer, who was briefed by Victor Gorlinsky on the night of the attack; and (11) Colonel Nathaniel P. Ward III US Army photo

I met Colonel Nathaniel P. Ward III, US Army, retired, on 7 August 1991, at an annual fund raiser for the Virginia Vietnam Veterans Memorial which was being built in Newport News. Colonel Ward explained to me that for six months he had been the Senior Corps Advisor in the Central Highlands, then Chief of Staff of the Vietnamese Command for twenty-six months, during the period when the 1959 attack happened. In less than a week, after our face to face conversation, I received a letter from him dated 11 August 1991, along with a short story from *USA Today* dated sometime in November 1982, the highlights of which read:

"But neither Buis' name nor the other American [Ovnand] was on the original list for the memorial..., because of a Defense Department directive issued in 1973.

"According to a Pentagon spokesman, the directive, written by the Pentagon comptroller, ordered that statistics of all combat casualties in the Southeast Asia theater begin on January 1, 1961. The directive didn't explain why that date was chosen, but it ignored previous deaths... [Colonel Ward] fired off an indignant letter to the Pentagon calling its attention to the deaths of the two American advisors...

"'I told them that a gross injustice would be committed if the names of these two honorable men were not included on the memorial,' said Ward."

Colonel Ward told me, "The story is basically correct except that I had to write eight or ten letters – not just one. I sent two to the Pentagon, several to different people connected with building the wall, and one to General Mike Davison, also involved with the memorial committee. I finally got a reply from General Davison (whom I knew slightly) to the effect that names would go back to include 1959!

"I launched my letter writing campaign because I felt so strongly about the war starting in the spring of 1959. There was a real hot war in Vietnam then – not attacking U.S. personnel until the Bien Hoa incident, but by guerillas and underground groups coming out from under cover. They were attacking Vietnamese Army camps. They'd walked right through army garrisons at night shooting things up. As the Chief of Staff of our Vietnamese Command, I knew of most of these attacks which ARVN headquarters reported to us."

Colonel Ward told me, "Generally, when new officers arrived, they received an initial briefing, basic rifle familiarization and a two-week orientation to Vietnam. In the case of Major Buis, his division was on an operation well north of Bien Hoa and he did not receive his two-week orientation, although I met him briefly when he processed in at Saigon."

Colonel Ward also said that Dale Buis was assigned to the 5th ARVN Division, well to the north of Bien Hoa, but could not remember the exact location, and he could not understand why Major Buis was at the BIF Compound on the night of the attack. He made no mention of Colonel Clay. Colonel Ward also mentioned specifics about muddy foot prints, and about the advisors waiting through the night for the bodies of Major Buis and Master Sergeant Ovnand to be picked up the following morning. He told me, "Many of our advisory compounds were soft targets."

In 1997, *Vietnam Military Lore - Legends, Shadows and Heroes* devoted twelve pages to the 1959 attack, but not all of what Colonel Ward had given me could be put into context at that time, although that changed in 2012, after speaking to LTC Victor Gorlinsky.

Colonel Ward passed away on 15 April 1998. After his death, I came to know his son, Nat, who was a first lieutenant with the 1st Cavalry Division's 2d Battalion, 8th Cavalry from January to May 1967. Nat lost his right foot, and the use of his left leg and hand, in an explosion while on recon on the Bong Son Plain, north of Qui Nhon. He was the first officer of the Vietnam War to be retained on active duty with such disabilities. I was surprised to learn that Nat was a teenager living in Saigon with his family on the night of the 1959 attack, and when his father was notified, and changed from khakis into fatigues as he readied himself to go to Bien Hoa, Nat wanted to tag along. His father empathically told him, "No!"

Since our first conversation, Nat and I have kept in touch.

In 2009 I was contacted by Dan Arant, a prodigious National Park Service volunteer who works at the Vietnam Veterans Memorial in D. C. Few volunteers are more knowledgeable, or more involved in the happenings at the Wall, than Dan. He asked me if I had any suggestions as to whom might qualify as guests at ceremonies for the 50th Anniversary of the deaths of Major Buis and Master Sergeant Ovnand. The subject of Major Howard Boston and LTC Victor Gorlinsky aside — I suggested Captain Nathaniel P. Ward IV and possibly members of Wentworth Academy, Dale Buis' old alma mater.

The 8 July 2009 ceremony at the Vietnam Veterans Memorial in Washington, D. C. Captain Nathanial Ward (left) and Major Sam Ratcliffe (right) hold photographs of Chester Ovnand and Dale Buis; as cadet Captain Joe Fowler; Greg Woodshed and Gordon Pavy look on. Photo by Donna Prince

Among guests at the 10:30 A.M. ceremony on 8 July 2009, were journalist Stanley Karnow; Nat Ward; the former commandant of Wentworth Military Academy Major Sam Ratcliffe; and a Wentworth honor guard.

On Friday, 10 July, Captain J. Errett Buis, USMC, sent an e-mail message to Jan C. Scruggs, "I am currently...stationed at headquarters Marine Corps...Arlington, Virginia...last night I caught news coverage of your...service for my father's uncle, Major Dale Buis, and Master Sgt Chester Ovnand... I wanted to thank you...especially given that there are American service members currently serving and sacrificing throughout the world. Memorial services, such as yesterday's, honor all service members who have sacrificed their lives for our country. On a personal note, I would like to express my gratitude for your efforts, as my brother, U.S. Army Specialist James V. Buis, also gave his life on 31 October 1998, at the age of twenty-four, while serving in Korea."

In April 2011 my wife Pia and I were invited to San Diego, California, to see the Wiedemann family, Bill, Betty, Marilyn and Joe, the family I had encountered, almost forty-five years ago, when I was assigned as the military escort to return their brother Bob's body home to Gary, Indiana. SP5 Robert J. Wiedemann, member of the 191st Military Intelligence Detachment, 1st Cavalry Division was killed during a rocket and mortar attack at Camp Evans on 25 March 1968. My wife and I spent much of our four days with Bill and his wife, Beverly, catching up on old times and speaking about things previously left unspoken. Bill asked me if there was anything I needed to do while in San Diego, and I mentioned that I

Author Ray Bows and Bill Wiedemann, brother of SP5 Robert J. Wiedemann, kneel by the gravesite of Major Dale R. Buis at Rosecrans Cemetery, San Diego, Calif. Pia Bows

wanted to pay my respects, and see Major Buis' grave and headstone at Rosecrans Cemetery out on Point Loma. Bill drove the four of us to the cemetery. There is no indication of Major Buis' service in Vietnam marked upon his headstone; nor is there any indication on the grave marker of Chester Ovnand's at Memorial Park Cemetery in Oklahoma City.

For the purpose of distributing benefits and burial, the government did not acknowledge American deaths in the Vietnam conflict until 5 August 1964. The date has since been changed to 28 February 1961, for veterans who served 'in Country.' Therefore, it appears those who served, solely in Vietnam at the time Major Buis and Master Sergeant Ovnand died, were not eligible for benefits as Vietnam veterans.

The veterans' benefits handbook in effect at the time of the attack on Bien Hoa was prepared by the 85th Congress, 2d Session (Title 38 – United States Code) on 15 September 1958, and put into effect on 1 January 1959. The handbook made provisions for living members of the Spanish-American War, the Philippine Insurrection, the Boxer Rebellion and those engaged in hostilities in Moro Province in the Philippines. Those dates were 21 April 1898 through 15 July 1903 inclusive. The other groups of veterans, also eligible, were those who had served in World War I, World War II, and Korea. The handbook made no mention of Vietnam.

Shortly after the Vietnam War, it was determined that any member of the Armed Forces of the United States who had served in Vietnam, or its contiguous waters or air space, was authorized to wear a bronze battle star on their Vietnam Service ribbon for each campaign in which they served. The Department of Defense recognized seventeen campaigns during the Vietnam conflict and the date 15 March 1962 was considered the beginning of the Advisory Campaign. The date was later changed to 28 February 1961, nineteen months and twenty days after the first deaths.

Chapter 22
No Matter Who Reads

Howard Boston, five years after his return from Vietnam. "Dad smiled for this photo," said his son Robert Boston. "He had finally gotten the feeling back in the right side of his face." Courtesy of Robert Boston

Victor W. Gorlinsky as a major with the 97th Signal Battalion, 7th Army in West Berlin, Germany 1961-1962 Courtesy of Blanche Gorlinsky

I always had the idea that Howard Boston's home could not be anything but a big white, two story house with a wrap around porch, and a nicely trimmed lawn with lots of elm trees. I am not sure if he had told me that, or not – but it was always my impression. He never wanted to talk much about himself, or the wounds he received at the Battle of the Bulge and in Vietnam. Almost everything I ever learned about Howard I have gotten from other sources - his son Bob, Vic Gorlinsky, and Howard's military record jacket under the Freedom of Information Act.

In the early 1990's we had many conversations over the phone. He would tell me the story of the 1959 attack as he dug back in his memory – I would take notes – write – then call and read to him – he would make corrections and then add a little more. When I located people who were relevant to the story, I'd call Howard to let him know what they had to say. Many participated, but it was Howard Boston who was the source for the story I wrote on Major Buis and Master Sergeant Ovnand as Chapter 6 in *Vietnam Military Lore – Legends, Shadows and Heroes.*

Howard B. Boston
6 February 1922 –13 May 1994
Courtesy of Robert Boston

One day in May 1994, I called and Ardys said, "Ray, Howard's gone. He passed away on the 13th." I was shocked because he never gave any indication that he was in anything but good health, and seemed active and happy right to his last days. After learning of his death, I dedicated Chapter 6 "The Saw Mill" to his memory. I wish that while Howard was alive, I could have called him and said, "Howard, I talked to Vic today." Regrettably, that would not happen until eighteen years after Howard died. Howard's wife, Ardys, born 11 July 1922, passed away on 13 December 2011. It is extraordinary having real friends that I had never met face to face, but who were voices on a telephone. As of this writing, Vic and I have not met face to face either, although we plan to link up in Washington, D. C. at the Vietnam Veterans Memorial in November 2012 for the 30th Anniversary of the Wall.

It has been seven months since I started working on this book and much has happened in that time. Vic Gorlinsky and I have talked on the telephone an average of once every other day since January 2012. He received my draft of the first twenty-one chapters on 23 July 2012, and made a few minor changes to the manuscript. By 27 July, the document was returned promptly with the note, "I've taken a little more time to review the manuscript, so it has been gone over completely twice. If you need more on anything, just let me know and we probably can clear it up on the phone or by e-mail."

In the final process, I asked Vic a few more questions about his family, and more about both his military and civilian careers. He furnished the following:

"The last time I saw Howard when I left Vietnam in April 1960, he was still assigned to Vietnam, but was under-going a check up at Clark Hospital in the Philippines. He met me at the Clark air terminal and we spent some time together before my connecting flight left. It was the last time I ever saw him.

"From there, I was sent to the Army Command and General Staff College at Fort Leavenworth, Kansas, for nine months, where I was promoted to major, and bumped into Major Charles Watson. After graduation, I asked to be assigned to Germany and arrived in Stuttgart in July 1961, just as the Berlin Wall was being built. The 'Cold War' was at its peak and I was assigned to the Seventh Army's 97th Signal Battalion as operations officer. A lot of time was spent on maneuvers and night work. In the spring of 1962, I was transferred to Heidelberg with the Signal Division of Headquarters U.S. Army Europe. I had the unusual job of inspecting the construction of communications facilities for NATO storage sites, located in all of the NATO countries. After two years, I moved to Karlsruhe where I took command of the 17th Signal Battalion.

Shortly after I arrived there in 1964, I was promoted to lieutenant colonel. I returned to Washington, D. C. in July 1965, and I was assigned to the Defense Communications Agency as a plans writer.

"I received orders for my second tour in Vietnam and arrived there in July 1968, almost nine years to the day after the Bien Hoa attack. I was assigned as the operations officer of Signal Division, Headquarters U.S. Army Vietnam (USARV). I worked and was billeted at Long Binh which was only a few miles from Bien Hoa. One time during my one year tour, I made it a point to get over to the old BIF Compound, which they had renamed for General William Train's son. I also learned that the Plaza Hotel had been named the Ovnand BEQ and the Buis Bachelor Officers Quarters had been named for our two losses. I never got to Saigon to see those sets of quarters, but at Bien Hoa I was surprised at how little the BIF Compound had actually changed. By then, security of the compound had been beefed up considerably. Old Bai, the cook, had lived with his family in a building next to our main building until we replaced him. His old quarters had been cleaned up, fitted with new shutters, and turned into a mail room and a separate field exchange (see illustration on page 9). There was also a formal mess hall, an officers' club, an enlisted club, a library, and a swimming pool. New advisory teams occupied the BIF. They performed functions as II Corps advisors and Bien Hoa Sector advisors. In touring the facility, I thought back to the days of good times and good friends, and of bad times and readjustment after the attack. My visit was brief, but certainly meaningful for me.

"I returned from Vietnam in July 1969, did a short stay at Sandia Base, New Mexico, and decided to retire after 30 years of military service. It was time for my wife, Blanche, and I to settle down. With our daughter, Vicki, married; our son, David, in college; and our youngest children, Paul, Barbara and Mark, in their teens and nearly ready for college; I found work in the civilian sector. I landed a job as manager with the Potomac Telephone Company and for eleven years handled a variety of jobs for the company, some of which involved such things as presidential inaugurations, the first visit of Pope John Paul II to the United States, and the Watergate Hearings."

The Plaza Hotel, 135 Tran Hung Dao, was officially named the Ovnand BEQ in 1965. US Army photo

The Buis BOQ, 13 Yet Kieu, was dedicated before July 1962 in memory of Major Dale R. Buis. I. Johnson

After the breakup of AT&T, Vic worked for several other communication companies and retired in December 1998, the month of his 75th birthday. His last assignment was holding the position of Senior Manager in the Special Projects Group at MCI Engineering.

It was through information passed on from Dan Arant to Vic Gorlinsky that, in January 2012, Vic visited Colonel Huynh Van Cao, the former commander of the 7th ARVN Division, at his home in Alexandria, Virginia. It was the first time they had seen each other since 1960. Colonel Cao now in his eighties, and although suffering from mild Alzheimer's, immediately recognized Vic and took both his hands in his own. The two men spoke softly to each other and looked into each others eyes, as memories of more than fifty years past ran through their minds. "For a long time we just stared at each other and watched tears of pain, happiness, and near forgotten memories stream down each others cheeks. I stayed about twenty minutes and promised I'd visit him again," said Vic.

Through the Vietnam Veterans Memorial Fund, it was arranged for Colonel Gorlinsky to be the first participant at the "Reading of the Names" ceremony on 7 November 2012, as part of the kick-off to the remembrances for the 30th Anniversary of the Vietnam Veterans Memorial in Washington, D. C. Vic was scheduled to read the names of Major Dale Buis and Master Sergeant Chester Ovnand, and I had promised to accompany him to the microphone and podium. During my research I located a DVD of the movie *The Tattered Dress.* Vic had never seen the movie in its entirety. On 2 August 2012, I loaned him my copy.

At 2330 hours, 12 August 2012, three hours ago, my cell phone rang, and looking at the number I thought to myself, *what a strange hour for Vic to be calling. Normally, we talk to each other much earlier in the day.* When I answered with, "Good evening, Colonel..." I heard Mrs. Gorlinsky's barely audible voice on the other end of the line, telling me that Vic had died suddenly at 1548 hours this afternoon. Only a few hours had passed from the time that he was stricken with pain in his chest until he took his last breath.

Lieutenant Colonel Victor Walter Gorlinsky
23 December 1923 - 12 August 2012
Courtesy of Blanche Gorlinsky

For me, it was as if Vic had completed all, but one, of his final missions. He had insured all the facts concerning the deaths of Major Buis and Master Sergeant Ovnand had been set straight, and he had finally seen *The Tattered Dress* in its entirety, after only having seen the first reel fifty-three years ago. The movie had begun at 1830 hours, 8 July 1959, and had been cut short by an event, forever etched in stone. Vic had done everything his country had asked of him . . . and more. It was as if his life had come full circle—almost.

Vic should have been at the 8 July 2009 ceremony, held for the 50th Anniversary of the deaths of Major Dale Buis and Master Sergeant Chester Ovnand, but it was not his fault. I failed to locate him. I should have looked harder, much harder, when Howard Boston had asked me to. Maybe, it wasn't completely my responsibility, but, still, I had failed.

Words cannot express the sense of sadness and loss that I feel for Vic Gorlinsky, who like Howard Boston, I only knew as a voice on the telephone. I'll miss the Colonel. Not nearly as much as those who knew him face to face, and the family who revered and loved him, but I will miss him none-the-less. Victor Gorlinsky was a part of history and I am proud to have called him my friend. We talked about things that had nothing to do with this book; about our families, and funny anecdotes, and close calls we had experienced; and about the good soldiers and the crazy characters we had met while stationed in the U.S. Army.

I feel privileged to have known both LTC Victor Gorlinsky and Major Howard Boston. I know that on this coming Veterans Day 2012, no matter who reads the first names inscribed on the Vietnam Veterans Memorial, I will be watching Howard and Vic mount steps to the podium at the apex of the Vietnam Veterans Memorial, together, to read two names in unison . . .

Dale R. Buis . . . .

Chester M. Ovnand. . . . . . .

EPILOGUE

There are many opinions about the "first American to die in Vietnam." Following in sequential order are some of the more significant circumstances.

On 10 May 1845, U.S. Navy Seaman William Cook died aboard the USS *Constitution* as it approached Tourane, Cochin China (Tourane would later become Da Nang). It was arranged by Captain "Mad Jack" Percival that Cook, a ship's musician, be buried on Tien Sha Peninsula and his grave be cared for by the Vietnamese in perpetuity. Three days after Cook's burial, it was learned that French missionary Bishop Dominique LeFevre was being held prisoner by Emperor Thieu Tri. In response, Mad Jack took three hostages, captured three armed junks, went ashore and ordered Marines to fire into crowds of people. He then fired on the fort which guarded the bay with "Old Ironsides'" two decks of cannons. After two weeks, Percival realized that he was being, tactically, outmaneuvered by the Vietnamese and departed Tourane, without gaining LeFevre's release.

William Cook's grave was cared for throughout the years, unbeknown to the thousands, upon thousands, of U.S. military who served in Vietnam. In April 2000, a team of Vietnam veterans located the grave and reported their findings in *Boston Globe* Magazine. Since the *Boston Globe* story, when people reach as far back in history as possible, because of the USS *Constitution's* first misguided military action in Vietnam, some say that Seaman William Cook was the first American to die there. However, he died of dysentery while out at sea, and although his remains are still at the base of Monkey Mountain, he does not qualify as "first to die in Vietnam."

Although Indochina remained quiet, as far as American military deaths for almost a century, U.S. Forces fought the Japanese in Vietnam during World War II. On 12 May 1942, pilot John T. Donovan, while with General Clair L. Chennault's Flying Tigers, dropped bombs on Hanoi's Gia Lam Airfield from his P-40 aircraft. After he strafed the airfield, Japanese anti-aircraft destroyed his plane and he was killed. Donovan was fighting Japanese Imperialism, not the communists. There have been some reports that in the 1940's a small group of U.S. Navy pilots had been executed, north of Saigon, after their aircraft had been shot down by the Japanese.

Project Embankment arrived in Saigon on 4 September 1945, with Colonel A. Peter Dewey, U.S. Army, as its commanding officer. The primary mission of the team was to locate some two-hundred American servicemen held at two Japanese prisoner of war camps in the Saigon area. Many of the Americans located by Colonel Dewey's team had been held in Burma for most of the war and were employed as slave laborers, building a railroad line that was to cross the Kwai River – the same group later made famous by the 1957 movie *Bridge on the River Kwai.*

Camp Poet in Saigon held five POW's, and Camp E-5, at the outskirts of the city, housed two-hundred-and-nine more American prisoners. Of these, one-hundred-and-twenty were from the 2d Battalion, 131st Field Artillery, 36th Division – National Guardsmen from Texas, who had been captured intact when they landed in Java by error – the unit became known as "The Lost Battalion". These prisoners suffered terribly at the hands of the Japanese and it is probable that some died in Vietnam.

Of the remaining POW's, eighty-six were survivors of the cruiser USS *Houston*, sunk on the night of 28 February 1942, off the coast of Java. Their fate had also been unknown until Colonel Dewey liberated them. The other eight men were airmen and sailors captured in the air and naval war with the Japanese in the skies and waters of Indochina between 1942 and 1945 – some had been captured during the bombing of Saigon Harbor, during a raid by American carrier-based-aircraft, during what was known as "The French Indochina Restraint". During all these military operations involving Americans, certainly, some had lost their lives, however, their names seem now known only to former comrades and their families.

On 26 September 1945, Colonel Dewey was driving his jeep as he approached a Viet Minh roadblock and barricade. He reduced his speed to five miles per hour as he swerved around the barrier, he noticed three Vietnamese in a roadside ditch. He shouted at them angrily in French, and they opened fire with a machinegun. Hit just behind his ear, Dewey was killed instantly. The first post World War II U.S. soldier killed in Vietnam, Colonel A. Peter Dewey's name is not inscribed on the Vietnam Veterans Memorial.

Nine years later, two American pilots flying for CAT (Civilian Air Transport) were killed at the Battle of Dien Bien Phu. They were Wallace A. Buford, of Salt Lake City, Utah, and James B. McGovern from Elizabeth, New Jersey. McGovern was known to most everyone as "Earthquake Magoon". They died the day before the French fortification fell on 7 May 1954, delivering supplies to the French, while piloting a "Flying Boxcar" when the airplane was hit by flak from a 37mm communist artillery shell.

On 29 April 1955, from a single engine flivver-plane, freelance photographer Everett Dixie Reese, a U.S. Army World War II veteran, was shot down and killed as he photographed the 20,000 strong Binh-Xueyen-Rebel-Army attacking Saigon, in an effort to overthrow Ngo Dinh Diem.

U.S. Air Force Technical Sergeant Richard B. Fitzgibbon, Jr., was the first American in Vietnam to be murdered by a fellow service member on 8 June 1956. While Fitzgibbon's name was added to the Vietnam Veterans Memorial on Panel 52E, line 21 in 1999, U.S. Air Force Staff Sergeant Edward C. Clarke, the man who murdered him, died while being chased by Vietnamese police after the murder. Clarke's name is not inscribed on the Wall for obvious reasons.

By 1957, the 1st Special Forces Group was sending training missions to Thailand, Taiwan and Vietnam. On 21 October 1957, during a training mission in Nha Trang an explosion took place which killed a U.S. Special Forces officer. The circumstances of the explosion have been surrounded by differences of opinion. Some are convinced that the explosion was a result of a communist mortar shell launched from the jungle, and that an enemy patrol had been stalking the trainees and their American advisors most of the day; while a majority of witnesses point to the fact that left over French Melinite being used by the American advisors caused the accidental explosion. No one denies that one night, shortly after Captain Harry Cramer's death, a mysterious explosion at the ammo dump destroyed the remainder of that Melinite – in place – so that it would take no further lives. Unlike the others wounded in Saigon on 22 October 1957, during three simultaneous bombings which injured Americans, when orders were finally issued on 7 May 1962 awarding Purple Hearts for those wounded in the autumn of 1957, no mention was made of Captain Cramer. His death had been deemed an accident. Even if Captain Cramer died at the hands of the communist, they were Viet Minh, not Viet Cong. The Viet Cong were not named as such until 1958. Captain Harry Cramer's name is inscribed on the Vietnam Veterans Memorial in Washington, D. C. on panel 1E, line 78.

On 4 April 1959, Major Stanley M. Staszak, a U.S. Army advisor to the Vietnamese Military Academy, Da Lat, died mysteriously in his sleep. His wife and two small children were stationed with him at the time.

While the press, historians, veterans groups and individuals ponder the question " Who was the first to fall in Vietnam?" there will continue to be gray areas about the distinction. One thing is for certain, M/Sgt Chester M. Ovnand and Major Dale R. Buis were the first two Americans to die at the hands of the Viet Cong in a premeditated attack, and are indeed the first two names on the Wall.

The 8 July 1959 attack was the first planned Viet Cong assault against American advisors using guerilla troops who were armed and expected to engage their U.S. enemy. Jan Scruggs and the founders of the Vietnam Veterans Memorial, thanks to Nathaniel P. Ward III, had gotten it right, from the Wall's conception. The beginning date of the Vietnam Conflict was 1959.

Glossary

ACSI	Assistant Chief of Staff , Intelligence
ADMSG	Administrative Message
AKA	Attack Cargo Ship - a flattop which carries vehicles
AMEMB	American Embassy
ASA	Army Security Agency
ASAP	As soon as possible
ARVN	Army Republic of Vietnam
BEQ	Bachelor Enlisted Quarters
BIF	*Bureau Industrielle Forestier* - the French Forestry Service
BOQ	Bachelor Officer Quarters
CAT	Civilian Air Transport
CG	Commanding General
CHMAAG	Chief MAAG
CIA	Central Intelligence Agency
CINCPAC	Commander in Chief Pacific Command
Class A	Military dress uniform
CO	Commanding Officer
COMSTOCK	Combat Support Tactical Operations Command Korea
CONUS	Continental United States
DEPTAR	Department of the Army
DMZ	demilitarized zone
ETA	Estimated time of arrival
ETD	Estimated time of departure

GHQ	General Headquarters
G I	Government Issue
KP	Kitchen Police
MAAG	Military Assistance Advisory Group
MAT-49	Sub machinegun — *Manufacture Nationale d'Armes deTulle*
MATS	Military Air Transport Service
MOS	Military Occupational Specialty
NATO	North Atlantic Treaty Organization
NCO	Non-Commissioned Officer
NOK	Next of Kin
OCS	Officer Candidate School
OQMG	Office of the Quartermaster General
POW	Prisoner of War
RIF	Reduction in Force
ROTC	Reserve Officers Training Corps
STEN	acronym for the weapons' chief designers—Major Reginald G. **S**hepherd and Harold **T**urpin - and **En**field
SNECMA	*Société Nationale d'Études et de Construction de Moteurs d'Aviation* (National Company for Design and Construction of Aviation Engines)
TAD	Table of Authorization and Distribution
TAG DA	The Adjutant General, Department of the Army
TERM	Technical Equipment Recovery Mission
UPI	United Press International
USARMA	United States Army Attaché
USARPAC	United States Army Pacific
USARV	US Army Vietnam
VC	Viet Cong
VE Day	Victory in Europe Day
WASHDC	Washington, DC

Bibliography

I. BOOKS

Bond, Rae, ed. *The Vietnam War: The Illustrated History of the Conflict in Southeast Asia.* Crown Publishers, 1979

Bowman, John S. et. al. *The Vietnam War, Day by Day.* Mallard Press, 1989

Bows, Ray A. *Vietnam Military Lore 1959-1973...Another Way to Remember.* Bows & Son, 1988

——. *Vietnam Military Lore - In The Name of War.* Bows & Son, 1996

——. *Vietnam Military Lore - Legend, Shadows & Heroes.* Bows & Son, 1997

Doyle, Edward, et. al. *The Vietnam Experience Series*, 21 vols, The Boston Publishing Company, 1981 (recommended reading)

Drake, Hal. *Pacific Stars and Stripes Vietnam Front Pages.* New York, Bonanza Books, 1986

Fleming, Ian. *Casino Royale.* London, Penguin Books, 2006

Ford, Daniel. *Flying Tigers: Claire Chennault and the American Volunteer Group.* Washington, Smithsonian Press, 1991

Hornfischer, James D. *Ship of Ghosts.* New York, Bantam Books, 2006

Karnow, Stanley. *Vietnam, A History: The First Complete Account of the Vietnam War.* New York, The Viking Press, 1983

Meyer, COL Harold J. "Jack". *Hanging Sam, A Military Biography of General Samuel T. Williams. From Pancho Villa to Vietnam.* North Texas Press, 1990

Newcomb, Richard. *A Pictorial History of the Vietnam War.* Doubleday & Company, Inc, 1987

Spector, Ronald H. *Advise and Support: The Early Years: The U.S. Army in Vietnam.* Washington, D. C. U.S. Army Center of Military History, 1985

Stein, Barry Jason. *U.S. Army Patches: An Illustrated Encyclopedia of Cloth Unit Insignia.* Columbia, South Carolina, University of South Carolina Press, 1997

Class Yearbook 1942 showing Junior College Sophomores. Wentworth Military Academy, May 1942

II. Government Publications

Marolda, Edward J. and Oscar P. Fitzgerald, *The United States Navy and the Vietnam Conflict: From Military Assistance to Combat, 1959-1965* Vol. 2, Navy History Divisions, Department of the Navy, 1976

III. Newspapers, periodicals and Articles

"American forces suffer first casualties in Vietnam", Oct 22, 1957, detached clipping
"Soldiers Injured as Bus Blown Up: Library, Hostel Hit" (AP), Oct 22, 1957, *Long Beach Press-Telegram*
"Two MAAG personnel, two Vietnamese Killed in Communist Attack", Daily Wireless File, *United States Information Service*, Saigon, 9 July 1959
"U.S, Aides Slain in Saigon – Billet Bombed by Terrorists", *Associated Press* (AP), 9 July 1959, detached clipping
"Viet Nam Seizes Suspects After 2 U.S. Soldiers Slain", *Fort Worth Telegram*, Fri, July 10, 1959
"2 U.S. Advisers Killed By Vietnam Communists", *United Press International* (UPI), Fri July 10, 1959, *The Stars and Stripes*
"Guard Hiked For Americans", *Associated Press* (AP), Saturday July 11, 1959, *The Stars and Stripes*
"Captain Saved Men in Attack", *United Press International* (UPI), undated clipping
"Vietnamese Raiders Kill 2 Americans", *Associated Press*, undated clipping
"Southeast Asia: Gunning at the Movies", *Newsweek*, July 20, 1959
"SOUTH VIET NAM: Death at Intermission Time", *Time* Magazine, July 20, 1959
"Sergeant Has Military Rites", *The El Reno American*, Reno Oklahoma, July 23, 1959
"U.S. Soldier Back in Vietnam", *New York Times*, Oct 4, 1959
"Our first Man to Die in Vietnam", *The Plain Dealer*, Cleveland, Ohio, May 29, 1972
"It took fight, but first to die is first on list", *USA Today,* November 10, 1982
"El Reno woman married to first killed in 'Nam", *El Reno Daily Tribune*, El Reno, Oklahoma, July 4, 1984
Rothschild, Richard. "It's a day to give thought to Dale Buis – His name may not be a household word, but the war he died in is", *The Houston Post*, July 8, 1984
"The 25th Anniversary of the First U.S. Death in Vietnam Calls Up a Legacy of Loneliness and Pride", article *People* Magazine, July 1984
Mulvey, Mike. "Nebraskan heads 'Nam memorial list," *Sunday Journal-Star,* Lincoln, Nebraska, July 1984
Mulvey, Mike. "Nebraskan heads 'Nam memorial list," *Sunday Journal-Star*, Lincoln, Nebraska, Sept 23, 1984
Arant, Dan. "Wall Notes," numerous issues, 2009 – 2012
Greilsamer, Alan. "Ceremony Honors First Vietnam Casualties", Press Release, *Communications Resources LLC*, July 1, 2009
"Benchmark Dates of the U.S. Advisory Phase of the Vietnam War", *VFW Magazine*, August 2011.
"Gen. Lang Presents Purple Heart To Widow of Late Maj Dale Buis", undated clipping
"Omaha Mother Proud", undated news clipping listing awards of Dale Buis.
"Early War Casualty Had Pender Roots", reprint from Nov 12 issue of Richmond, Va. *News Leader,* – news clipping no year.
Camp McCauley, NCO Academy undated story – source unknown
Chester M. Ovnand, Wikipedia, free encyclopedia [Online] Available at http:// www.en.wikipedia.org/wiki/Chester_M._Ovnand
Naylor, William E. Col. USAF (ret.). "My Memories of Dale Buis", December 27, 1998 [Online] Available at http:// www.vvmf.org/thewall/anClip=2825
Kneisel, Peter. "Searching For The Lost Grave.." article in *The Boston Globe (*Magazine), Boston, MA, 29 Oct 2000

IV. Unpublished Documents

Unofficial Trial Transcript by Victor Gorlinsky, 29 December 1959 (4 pages)
Letter from Dale Buis to family members, 22 April 1959, 3 pages
Unpublished letter from Virginia Buis to Gretchen Buis dated 9 July 1978 (9 pages).
Letter from Gertrude Essex Knudson to Gretchen Buis, dated September 8, 1986
Telephone conversations with U.S. Marine Joe Atkinson in the summer of 1988
Letter from Edward M. Mayzel, USMC 1808640 detailing his time in Okinawa and off shore in Vietnam in 1959, dated 6 May, 1988
Letter from Edward M. Mayzel, USMC 1808640 with additional details about his time in Okinawa and off shore in Vietnam in 1959, dated 4 January 1991
Letter from Col. Nathaniel P. Ward III to M/Sgt Ray Bows detailing Ward's attempts and success in placing Buis and Ovnand's names on Vietnam Veterans Memorial, 11 August 1991.
Vietnam 1959, unpublished speech notes by LTC Victor Gorlinsky, July 2008, (3 pages)

Letter to Ray Bows from Victor Gorlinsky, 31 December 2011 subject Vic's first tour in Vietnam
Letter from Victor Gorlinsky dated 1 Jan 2012 subject: group down to four.
"My Military Service History", unpublished document by LTC Victor Gorlinsky, undated
Howard B. Boston's releasable military records under the Freedom of Information Act
Dale R. Buis' releasable military records under the Freedom of Information Act
Hqs, DA, Wash DC General Order 24 Posthumous Purple Heart Award Buis & Ovnand
MAAG Vietnam Message Traffic July 1959 – numerous transmissions
Final Pay Roll Record of Ninth Company Officers Candidate School, Fort Knox, Kentucky for Chester M Ovnand
Report of Death, DA Form 52-1 dated 14 July 1959 for Chester M. Ovnand
Restricted Extract of Special Orders 131 dated 1 June 1944 ref: Chester Melvin Ovnand
Hqs Oklahoma Military District, letter AKMOK-5 201, 28 Oct 1952, applying to Chester M. Ovnand appointment in Officer's Reserve Corps.
Unpublished notes "Reconstruction of the VC Attack on the BIF Compound" based on telephone conversations between Major Howard Boston and Ray Bows (April 1993 to May 1994) and telephone conversations between LTC Victor Gorlinsky and Ray Bows (January 2012 to August 2012) containing the most plausible theory as to how the VC arrived at BIF by boat and positioned themselves around the building before the firing started.
Unpublished document of LTC Robert D. McKnight, USA (ret.); LTC Infantry MI and PSYOP Special Forces
Unpublished 1959 Conference notes of Colonel Bergen B. Hovell, commander
Notes from Dan Arant dated 11 September 2012 references to John T. Donovan and "The Lost Battalion."
Department of the Army Casualty Information System List, US Department of the Army
United States Army Enlistment Records - Armed Forces of the United States. DD Form 4 Record Enlistment and DD Form 1300Report of Casualty, 1961 to 1969
United States Army Vietnam General Orders (1965-1969). US Department of the Army, Awards and Decorations Branch, Washington, DC

VI. Archival Sources

National Archives, Washington, DC

Washington National Records Center, Suitland, MD
John Fitzgerald Kennedy Library, Boston, MA
Lyndon B. Johnson Presidential Library, Austin, TX

US Department of the Army

Awards and Decoration Branch, Washington, DC
Memorialization Branch, Washington, DC
US Military History Institute, Carlisle Barracks, PA
JFK Special Warfare Center, Fort Bragg, NC
West Point Military Archives, West point, NY
Office of the Post Historian, Fort Myer, VA

US Department of Defense

Office of Public Information, Press Branch
US Military Records Center, St. Louis, MO

US Department of the Navy

Operational Archives Branch, Naval Historical Center, Washington Navy Yard, DC
History and Museums Division Headquarters, US Marine Corps, Washington, DC

National Personnel Records Center

Military Personnel Records, 9700 Page Avenue, St. Louis, MO 63132-5100

VII. Interviews, Personal Papers and Photos

Our sincerest gratitude to the following individuals who shared their time, personal papers and photographs.

Daniel R. Arant; historian, Vietnam veteran and National Park Service Volunteer
Mike Arman; author and publisher (M. Arman Publishing)
Frances Armstrong; daughter of Major Howard Boston
Joe Atkinson; U.S. Marine stationed with the 3d Marine Division
Dennis Badore and Doris Crary; far away friends close to our hearts
Hon. J. Stephen Buis; nephew of Major Dale R. Buis
Major J. Errett Buis, USMC; son of Hon. J. Stephen Buis
Gretchen Buis; Buis family historian and relative of Major Dale R. Buis
Kurt Buis; son of Major Dale R. Buis
Ardys A. Boston; wife of Major Howard Boston
Major Howard B. Boston, US Army (ret.); member of MAAG 7
Robert Boston; son of Major Howard Boston
Tom Conroy; Hollywood Movie Stills
LTC Hank Cramer, US Army (ret.); son of Captain Harry Cramer, Jr.
David Do; Vietnamese translator
Don Durham Sr.; Wentworth Military Academy classmate of Dale R. Buis
Duery Felton, Jr.; B/1/2 Inf, 1st ID, 1967/ Curator, Vietnam Veterans Memorial Collection
Robert Fitch; member of MAAG Indochina/Vietnam and contributor of info on Everett D. Reese
Blanche Gorlinsky; wife of LTC Victor Gorlinsky
Lieutenant Colonel Victor W. Gorlinsky, *US Army (ret.);* member of MAAG 7
*Col. John D. Howard, US Army (ret.);*Senior Military Advisor, Go Cong Province, VN 1968-1970
Ray Jewett; MAAG Public Information Office photographer
I. Johnson; Vietnam veteran and contributor of photographs
Joanne J. Jones; research librarian, Massasoit Community College, Brockton, Massachusetts
CW4 Mitsugi Kasai, US Army (ret.); served with Dale R. Buis
Barbara E. Keith; contributor of unpublished documents of Robert D. McKnight
Peter Kneisel; reporter for *The Boston Globe*
Edward M. Mayzel; contributor of maps and charts USMC #1808640
Betty Menard; sister of SP5 Robert J. Wiedemann
David Mitchell; Memorial Park Cemetery, Oklahoma City, OK
Col William E. Naylor USAF (ret.); served with Dale R. Buis in Japan
R. William "Bill" Pratt; SP5 USA MAAG Vietnam, stationed in Saigon from 1956 to 1958
Donna Prince; National Park Service Volunteer & photographer
Linda Rutty; Volusia County, Florida librarian
Jan C. Scruggs; Vietnam Veterans Memorial co-founder
P. Mike Seuberling; former police instructor, University of Miami, Florida
John Sheridan; nephew of M/Sgt Chester M. Ovnand
Robert J. Sloan; member of 27th Infantry Division WWII
Mickey Speck; contributor of photographs
Bruce Swander; historian; former U.S. Marine, Vietnam 1966-1970
Lee Schwartz; research librarian, Marion County, Florida
Robert F. and Kathy A. Walker; think-tank consultants
JoAnn Waller; Vietnam Veterans Memorial Fund
Colonel Nathaniel P. Ward III, US Army (ret.); Chief of the Vietnamese Staff, MAAG
Captain Nathaniel P. Ward IV, US Army (ret.); son of Colonel Nathaniel P. Ward III
Kenneth Whick; former U.S. Marine
Bill and Beverly Wiedemann; brother and sister-in-law of SP5 Robert J. Wiedemann
Joe Wiedemann; brother of SP5 Robert J. Wiedemann
Marilyn Wiedemann; sister of SP5 Robert J. Wiedemann

And thank you Harper Scotti Bows and Scarlett Lovely Bows, DJ Hunter Bows, Alessia and Natalia, Mia Grace, and Nathan, for spreading joy into our lives.

Index